So Your Wife Came Home Speaking in Tongues?

So Did Mine!

Robert Branch

So Your Wife Came Home Speaking in Tongues?

So Did Mine!

Fleming H. Revell Company
Old Tappan, New Jersey

All Scripture quotations in this volume are from the Revised Standard Version of the Bible, copyrighted 1946 and 1952.

Library of Congress Cataloging in Publication Data

Branch, Robert.
    So your wife came home speaking in tongues? So did mine!

    Bibliography: p.
    1. Glossolalia--Case studies. 2. Branch, Robert.
I. Title.
BL54.B67   248'.29   73-7521
ISBN 0-8007-1610-2
ISBN 0-8007-0611-0 (pbk.)

Contents

So Your Wife Came Home Speaking in Tongues?

So Did Mine!

1

You're Married to An Angel!

"Is everybody ready? Okay then, let's try it out. But go slowly!"

The powerful whine of overhead hoists suddenly filled the spacious workroom as two ponderous steel assemblies started moving toward an apparent rendezvous. "Steady now! Slowly, go slowly. That's it. How about it, are they lining up?"

An assistant in white coveralls emblazoned with corporate insignias leaned over and peered intently at the closing interface. Several indecisive seconds ticked away as the gap grew smaller, smaller. Finally he straightened, grinned, and yelled, "Hey, yeah! They're gonna make it this time! Good job, Bob!"

I smiled at the rare compliment and breathed a sigh of relief. "Close it up and secure it, then. Looks like we all get to go home on time tonight!"

Engineers are like everyone else; they feel great when they do a good job. And what a difference it makes in your work, I reflected, to have peace of mind.

The day's grime yielded to a good scrubbing with

soap and water. Presentable again, I slipped into my jacket and closed the door on my workaday world of metals, ceramics, and plastics. Outside, however, I had to stop and blink at the brilliance of the spring afternoon.

Barbara and I had come to this small southwestern city ten years before precisely because of its climate, but I never ceased to be amazed at the jewellike days it could produce. This early May day was one of those. Our massive mountains to the east stood out in crisp detail in the unpolluted high-altitude air. Breezes carried pine resin aromas to my nostrils as my eyes focused slowly on the cholla cactus and multicolored tulips decorating our factory grounds. Overhead, jet contrails bleached narrow streaks across a cloudless blue sky.

"Hey, Bob! Won't your wife let you come home tonight?"

I clenched a fist in feigned anger at my joshing friend, but turned and started for the parking lot anyway. It was also nice at home these days; why kill time getting there?

It takes about twenty-five minutes to drive from the factory to our house at the foot of the mountains, and I usually took advantage of this time to do a lot of thinking. Today, after I had nosed my pickup into the departing chain of vehicles, my mind wandered back over the events of the past three months. What a trial they had been, and how nice to have them behind me!

The period had started with high hopes and bold actions. In February, a stockbroker had called about an exciting new star rising in the housing industry. Barbara had left the decision to buy into the venture with me. Was it a good investment for our modest savings? I thought it was, so I invested heavily. Since it was such a *good* opportunity, I also bought shares for the kids, using money their grandfather had given them for future college days. Then I had sat back to watch the profits pour in.

A month went by and the price of the stock was suddenly cut in half. The stockbroker assured me, however, that nothing was *fundamentally* wrong. "Just sit tight, Bob, and it will correct itself," he had advised. But the very next month, after a quick series of jarring drops, the company declared bankruptcy and it was all over, just like that.

Frantically, I called my broker and he told me a tale of withheld payments, loose accounting practices, false press releases, and mismanagement. "I'm sorry, Bob," he had lamely concluded. *He* was sorry! Our savings, the kids' money—all gone in less than two months!

I talked to our lawyer about possible suit, but he said there was insufficient legal basis. "It's really too bad, Bob, but there's nothing you can do."

If you've ever known guilt in your own life, you can imagine how I felt then. It had been *my* decision to buy the stock, and a good deal of the lost money really hadn't belonged to me. A second bankruptcy now occurred, the bankruptcy of Bob Branch's spirit. I sank into a depression so dark and so deep Barbara became very anxious.

"I don't *care* about the money, darling," she had said. "We'll make that back somehow. But you've got to quit blaming yourself. This *gloom* is tearing you up and spilling over onto us. I'm really worried about you."

It had been like a nightmare. I could hear her talking, I knew she was right, but I couldn't seem to quit hating myself. Finally, though, the turning point had come and it was Barbara who found the key.

"There's going to be a retreat, Bob, and I think we should go. If you could just quit thinking about this thing for awhile, you'd feel better. Please go with me?"

That had been the previous weekend. No one knew of my personal problem except Barbara, but much of what was said seemed aimed directly at me. As the hours passed there in the mountain lodge, I could feel myself gradually relaxing. Finally, the grip of melancholia released completely and I silently accepted God's forgiveness. With His forgiveness, I was free to forgive myself and I wish I could describe the sense of relief that came! I dismounted my self-made cross and sort of gurgled back to life.

Well, this was the following Thursday and I was still marveling at the restorative powers available to Christians. It had been a wonderful week at work and at home. Without getting uptight, I was even making plans to replace the lost money.

I swung the pickup into our new development. Already neighbors were out working—setting out long-needled pine trees, forming flower beds and retainers with porous black lava rock, bordering grass areas with gracefully curving redwood lathing, installing lawn plumbing—all the things required to transform pebbly desert plots into pools of beauty. As I pulled into the driveway, I was pleased with the effect of our new landscaping that we had slaved over together the previous autumn.

Barbara met me at the door with Jerry, nine, and Judy, seven, close on her heels. "Hi!" she said simply, hugging me with the extra warmth I'd noticed (and enjoyed) all week. Unlike those days of withdrawal, I hugged her back, holding on capriciously until she broke my grip with a teasing little laugh.

The noise level at the dinner table would have damaged a bachelor's ears. After Jerry said grace with his customary boyish haste, everyone launched into overlapping stories that just had to be told. Added to the clink of silverware on china and a forgotten TV in the next room, the result must have sounded like stereo gone wild! But I enjoyed it nevertheless. This was *life* as it should be.

Finally, however, the day's fatigue must have shown because Barbara said to me, "I don't think you feel like going out tonight."

I shrugged. "Sure I do. Besides, what would the PTA do without me?"

"Listen, Katherine Moffat is going to be there and I haven't talked to her since we went bowling together last fall, remember? Why don't I go and you get those wrinkles off your face?"

"That's not fair; you had to go the last time!" But I hoped she'd insist.

She did, bless her heart! "Shut up! It's settled."

So by eight o'clock, Barbara was off to the meeting and I had the kids bathed and in bed. Graciously, they didn't make comparisons as I read a Bible story and listened to their prayers, tasks usually performed by their mommy. I kissed Judy and ruffled Jerry's blond hair. As the light went out on their smiling faces, I thought how lucky I was to have them.

It was still too early to go to bed. I stood for awhile at the front door letting the soft evening breeze wash over me. I *was* tired and didn't feel like doing any garage projects. But what to do? And then I remembered the book Frank Beecham had thrust on me. Maybe I should start reading it.

I didn't want to, really, but Frank was our Sunday-school leader and Barbara was a good friend of Frank's wife, Celia. We had attended the first meeting of a new Bible study group at their house just the night before when Frank had given me the book. He expected to get my opinion on it.

I retrieved it now and looked with distaste upon its cover—*They Speak With Other Tongues* by John Sherrill. Ugh! But Frank wanted me to read it for some reason.

This was not a neutral subject with me; I had been solidly opposed to it since boyhood days. I couldn't understand why it seemed to hold such interest for some now. With increasing frequency I was hearing it mentioned.

For example, about six weeks before, Barbara had started attending a Thursday morning prayer group. After the first meeting, she had commented to me,

"Some of the women were speaking in tongues. Now I'm not sure what I think about that. But there was real joy at that meeting, Bob; I wish you could have seen it! People were saying 'Praise the Lord!' without any embarrassment whatsoever. And we sang fast, peppy songs of praise, not at all like those dirges in church. It was marvelous!"

Obviously, she had enjoyed it and I'd seen nothing sinister in what she had described. Members of many church denominations were in this particular group, including several of Barbara's friends from our own church. So what if some of the other women believed in tongue speaking? Barbara had a college degree and had taught school for five years. She wasn't going to be drawn into such an offbeat doctrine. At that time, I had been much more concerned about the lost savings.

But at the retreat it had come up again. It was the one discordant note for me during the entire weekend. Somehow a discussion got started about the charisma, or gifts, of the Holy Spirit. There was, it seemed, some sort of movement in progress that emphasized these gifts and it had been tagged the Charismatic Movement. Murray Simms, our retreat leader, related an incident in which a teen-ager had accused him of not possessing the Holy Spirit because he didn't speak in tongues. Anyone who knew Murray at all would have had to laugh at such a ridiculous accusation. The discussion continued, nevertheless, long past the point of holding my interest. Why spend so much time on nonessentials, I thought as I fidgeted, especially on one so far out? It didn't seem to bother Barbara, however.

Finally there had been a break, and we had all filtered outside among the pine and spruce, the juniper and cactus. Frank had come up to me, his face alight with enthusiasm. "What do *you* think of speaking in tongues, Bob?"

Trying not to sound harsh, I had replied, "I don't believe in them. I've seen what they can do to people and I've seen them turn other people away from God. No sir, I don't believe in them."

Frank had persisted. "Maybe you just saw them abused. Why don't we go to a Pentecostal prayer meeting at the university some night? You might get an entirely different impression."

I liked Frank. He, Murray, and I all worked for the same company. But I didn't like the course of this conversation. With as much diplomacy as I could muster, I told him not to call me—I'd call him. Thankfully, I wasn't involved with this freaky little movement and I didn't want to be.

That should have ended it, I thought, but the night before, Frank had literally shoved this book into my hands. The group purportedly was going to study the Book of Mark. Everyone in attendance belonged to our own Protestant church which was non-Pentecostal. What possible relationship could a book on speaking in tongues have to *this* group?

Still, I had some time on my hands this evening, and possibly if I read the book, I could settle the issue once and for all. The cushion on my wingback chair gave a sigh of expelled air as it received my weight, a sigh I matched as I reluctantly flipped the pages to chapter one.

This was to be the last time for several weeks that I would start reading a book so casually. John Sherrill is an excellent writer and he very quickly drew me into the story he had to tell. And what a story it was! He took me by the hand and started showing me another world, a world that existed all around me that I hadn't seen. In some it would have torched flames of excitement; in me it set off clanging bells of alarm!

The Charismatic Movement, I learned, didn't involve hundreds of people as I'd thought, but hundreds of *thousands,* perhaps even millions. It wasn't confined to one geographical area, but had spread from coast to coast and into many foreign countries. It didn't concern only one group of churches, but had adherents in *all* mainline Protestant denominations and even the Roman Catholic church. All kinds of people were becoming involved, representing all educational and occupational categories. And it seemed to be gathering momentum with each passing day.

Sherrill explained the Baptism in the Holy Spirit, an experience I'd heard reference to at the retreat without fully understanding. Clearly, this experience is central to the Charismatic Movement. During the Baptism in the Holy Spirit, most people begin speaking in unknown tongues. Therefore, not a small fraction of the people involved in the Movement speak in tongues, but practically *all* of them do! Millions, perhaps; a vast *army* of tongue speakers!

I'd had no idea I'd been on the fringe of something so big. How many people, I started wondering, were involved in this movement in our city? How many people were involved in our church, and who were they? At this point, a new and horrible suspicion took root in my mind. Oh no, not Barbara—not my own wife!

Whatever peace I had felt when I left the factory, whatever contentment I had experienced around the dinner table, was gone now. As quickly as a lake's surface is broken by the winds of storm, my soul's quiescence was shattered by this repugnant possibility. My mind groped for evidence.

Barbara had said *some* of the women in her prayer group spoke in tongues. Some—or all? Funny that she'd never mentioned that aspect of the meetings again. Then that last night of the retreat we had closed by singing fast-paced gospel songs. With unusual enthusiasm, Barbara had clapped her hands briskly in time with the music and had swayed slightly from side to side as she sang, exactly as several others around the room were doing. Was this significant? She had raised no protest when Frank had urged me to go to a Pentecostal meeting, nor when he pressed Sherrill's book upon me. But most of all, I thought about that puzzling incident of the night before at the Bible study meeting.

We had completed the first twenty verses of the first chapter of Mark, and, as coffee was being served, had drifted off into a discussion of the Apostles' Creed. I remarked that I understood everything in that affirmation of faith except the phrase "the communion of saints." "Does *saints* mean living Christians in the sense used in the New Testament? Or does the phrase mean communication between living and dead Christians? I've never been sure."

No one else had seemed to know either.

"Well, if it does mean communication with the departed," I'd continued, "I wonder what sort? How do we talk to angels?"

At this, Celia Beecham brightened. "Why Bob," she'd said, smiling broadly as her eyes darted between Barbara's and mine, "you're *married* to one!"

I had laughed good-naturedly with the others at first, but it soon became apparent that I must have missed something the others had heard. The chuckling continued. Several of the women were staring at Barbara with beaming faces. Color had crept into Barbara's face and she had lowered her eyes, though still smiling. I had been at a loss for comment so I also smiled, but by then somewhat nervously.

Now I sat in our den knowing I had a question to ask. Only the measured ticking of our mantel clock and the sounds of breathing from the children's bedroom broke the stillness. I felt tense and apprehensive. I thought I already knew the answer. And at about that moment, Barbara arrived home.

Conversation about the PTA meeting evaporated quickly as Barbara's eyes kept being drawn to the book in my lap. "I see you've been reading Sherrill's book," she ventured. "What do you think of it?"

"I . . . uh . . . well, Sherrill's style is very easy to read." Mentally I kicked myself for that evasion! Difficult questions stick to the throat like flesh to cold metal.

With great effort, I forced it up. "Barbara, I have to ask this. Have *you* started speaking in tongues?"

I'll never forget the look on her face at that moment. It was a portrait of quiet joy. Her eyes sparkled, her lips broadened into a peaceful smile before parting briefly to say "Yes," as tenderly as if she'd softly kissed me.

My stomach grabbed sharply. Still I managed to ask, "When did you start?"

"A week ago, at the morning prayer group meeting. The day before the retreat."

My throat closed and I could say no more. I sat there and stared at my wife in disbelief. Her face was angelic as she started telling me details of her own Baptism in the Holy Spirit, details I barely heard for the irrational throbbing that had started in my head. A week before I hadn't heard of the Charismatic Movement—tonight it had exploded in my face! Aftershocks would be felt for a long time to come!

2

Declaration of War

Barbara couldn't know of the huge amounts of adrenaline shooting through my body in those moments after my questions. She talked on as my heart pumped faster and faster, demanding some sort of action. I couldn't just sit there!

She was in midsentence as I jumped up and rushed out of the house into the backyard. Welcome darkness closed around me as I started a furious pacing pattern, back and forth from fence to fence. After five strenuous minutes, I slowed down a bit, feeling some relaxation in my overtaut muscles. For the first time, I noticed there was no moon in the night sky. The stillness was broken only by the distant barking of some excited dog. I continued to pace, but more slowly now.

My mind balked at logical thought. Like a supermarket clerk whose canned goods display had just been toppled, I didn't know where to start to restore mental order. I walked some more.

Out of the past, a picture floated into my mind, a remembrance from high-school days. I was in bed in my upstairs room. All the windows were raised in an effort to defeat the humid, stifling, summer heat. I tried to sleep but couldn't. Through the open windows came sounds, strange sounds, haunting sounds. Two and one-half blocks away, a Pentecostal meeting was still going on at a local college sanctuary. It had been three hours now, and the sounds had only increased in variety, volume, and frenzy. A pillow over my head gave temporary relief, but it was too hot to continue that solution for very long. I wished they would quit. Suddenly, I heard the sharp slaps of shoe leather on pavement. I raised up on one elbow quickly, just in time to see a young man run past on the sidewalk below. His arms were pumping and his head was thrown back as he hurtled down the street. But to where? This was a residential neighborhood—there were no all-night stores open, no buses to catch. I looked at the clock. It was after midnight.

Another scene from that same period now crowded into my mind. It was a Saturday afternoon and I was working my part-time job at the downtown movie theater. On the opposite corner, a group of students from that same college were conducting a street meeting. Some farmers had gathered, listening to the accordion music and the singing. A young man, waving one hand in the air while balancing an open Bible in the other, started preaching loudly. After only a few minutes, another male student suddenly started making loud unintelligible noises and shaking. He sank to the pavement and lay there, his body apparently rigid except for his extremities which were twitching. After some delay, his friends lifted him into a car and drove away.

How many nights during those years was I denied sleep by those frightening noises? How many Saturdays had I observed those passionate street meetings? How many stories were circulated about the Pentecostals and the strange goings-on at their college?

I shook my head violently to drive out the memories. But I couldn't dislodge one fact—*all the Pentecostals had spoken in unknown tongues!* And now my own wife was doing it!

The evening coolness started reminding me I had bolted outside without a jacket. I returned to the den. Barbara hadn't moved, and I was surprised to see my irregular behavior hadn't visibly upset her. It was almost as if she had expected it.

"Feel better?" she asked calmly.

"A little."

"Bob, I know what you're thinking and it isn't like that at all. Our meetings are very controlled. Everything is done in good order, just like the Bible says they should be. There's no shaking or rolling or anything like that. Really, it's all very beautiful and joyous."

Barbara had lived some of her life in the same hometown, but her house had been considerably farther from the college than ours. Besides, she had spent her high-school days in another town.

"Why didn't you tell me before now? Were you hoping to keep it a secret?"

"No, but I thought I knew what would happen and I was waiting for a good time. And I was right, wasn't I?" I winced.

"It's in the Bible, Bob. Paul says he wishes that all of us would speak in tongues. But that's not all of it. Many people have been healed by the prayers of this group. Miraculous healings! Now, *our church* should be preaching and doing that, but it's not. Our church isn't preaching the whole Bible."

I was becoming unnerved by my inability to adequately counter what she was saying. So I lamely asked, "Who else is involved in this? The speaking in tongues?"

Very calmly, she started naming people. Almost all the young adults we knew in our church, practically all of the people at the retreat, 75 percent of the people in our Sunday-school class and in the Bible study group. More unnerving still, she also named four neighborhood women living on our block alone, who were not members of our church at all.

Now I knew part of the reason for her calmness. She was literally surrounded with people who believed in this doctrine. Could so many be wrong? But if she was comforted by so large a group of supporters, I was more alarmed than ever. My mind staggered under the weight of so much revelation in one night.

Barbara started speaking again, but I stopped her. "No! No, I don't want to talk about it anymore tonight. I need to finish reading this book before I say anymore. And I think I'll do that right now!"

She smiled her assent, still perfectly composed and comfortable. I marveled at this in spite of my turmoil; Barbara had always been a very emotional woman in keeping with her Irish ancestry. Tonight, our normal roles were reversed.

I tried to return to Sherrill's book as Barbara readied herself for bed, but the sounds came back. Over the years, they moaned and stuttered and wailed at me. Now they were joined by new sounds of mocking and taunting laughter. Imaginary voices cried, "You're married to an angel, Bob!" and, "His own wife is speaking in tongues and he doesn't even know it!" A choir of church members and neighbors looked down on me in glee.

My eyes blurred with tears. Throwing the book down, I left the house again, this time going to my pickup. I remember seeing Barbara's face at the bedroom window as I roared off down the street.

It wasn't a matter of going anywhere in particular, but simply of grinding out overwhelming emotion by the mere process of going. At one point, I found myself parked in front of our darkened church buildings staring at the crosses silhouetted against the night sky. Later, I was on a freeway hurtling north to nowhere. I prayed aloud, practically shouting at times. "*Why,* Lord? Why? Haven't I taught for you? Haven't I tithed? Haven't I sought your daily guidance? Haven't I made retribution for past mistakes? Why, Lord, why this?"

An hour and a half after I left, I pulled back into our driveway, miraculously safe and emotionally drained. Inside, the house was still and quiet. The rest of the night I spent in our living room with Sherrill's book and the Bible—reading, checking, trying to think.

When darkness finally yielded to the first light of morning, I had finished and I was very, very tired. It was Friday, a workday. I prayed for strength to face the day without sleep.

It was too late to discuss the book with Barbara, so I mumbled something about talking that evening and left the house. I'll never know how I got through that day. My memory of it is as blank as I felt. Somehow, though, it passed, I got home safely, and ate all the dinner I could stomach, which wasn't much. Finally the moment came when I had to talk to my wife.

"Barbara," I proclaimed, "until now we've been in perfect agreement on religious matters. For the most part, you've led and I've followed, and I didn't mind following because I believed you were right. But I cannot accept this speaking in tongues. On this point, I will *not* follow you. I realize I have no right to tell you not to do it yourself. But we may as well accept this fact, that we have reached a dividing point in our beliefs and that from now on we walk different paths."

For the first time, a hint of alarm appeared in her eyes. "It doesn't have to be that way, Bob. There is really no reason. . . ."

"No," I stopped her. "I realize I'm about to pass out with fatigue, but I know what I'm saying. I don't believe in tongues. And there's something else I want to say before I go to bed. I don't want to go to any Pentecostal meetings. If we go to any other meeting and someone unexpectedly starts speaking in tongues, I'll get up and walk out. I don't want your prayer group meeting in our house. I don't want to hear *you* speaking in tongues. And I sure don't want you teaching it to our kids! That's the way I feel about it and I can't help it. After I've had some sleep, I'll discuss it with you, if you like, but after this weekend, I don't want to hear about it anymore." With that bit of chauvinism out of my system, I sort of staggered out of the room, flopped onto the bed, and immediately passed out.

It was, of course, a declaration of war. But I was too tired, too hurt, and too scared to care.

3

Lost Weekend

Saturday morning, May 6, dawned in shimmering brightness. I blinked my eyes as I suddenly came awake and quickly checked the clock. 6:45! One leg jerked out from under the cover before I realized I didn't have to go to work. Sighing, I sank back onto the pillow.

Barbara stirred briefly beside me and I looked over at the lump of cover that I knew concealed my wife. She always slept with her head covered, a carry-over from chilly childhood mornings in a house with no central heating. Her form became still again and she continued to sleep.

Remembering now my speech of the night before, I eased out of bed, slipped on a robe, and headed for the kitchen. I didn't want any discussion to start before I'd had some coffee!

It took two cups to blow out the cobwebs of the extra-long night's sleep. After allowing Johnnything, our demanding little dog, to have his time in the yard, I refilled my cup and poured another for Barbara. Jerry and Judy brushed past me with a quick, "Hi!" as I moved back toward our bedroom. Saturday-morning cartoons would glue them to the TV for the next several hours, I knew.

There *would* be a talk. Barbara and I had always enjoyed talking with one another. We discussed everything—our plans, our memories, our religion, our kids' behavior, home improvements, jobs, sports, politics, everything—for hours at a time. We often laughed at ourselves that one time we had spent all day long simply talking, without ever getting dressed! Secrets had been unknown around our house—until now. And that really ate at me.

I sat at the desk while Barbara propped herself up in bed and drank her coffee. She studied me as I sat silently sulking. She was calm, but not placid, and I could tell the irish was building up inside her.

Finally she asked, "Did you really mean those things you said last night?"

I set my jaw. "Yes."

"That's being pretty narrow-minded, wouldn't you say?"

"No, I *wouldn't* say that. It's just the way I feel about it, that's all. You have the right to take up this 'thing' if you want to, but I have an equal right not to have anything to do with it."

Her eyes flashed. "This 'thing'? Oh, Bob, you call yourself a Christian and you can talk that way? Why, you make it sound . . . dirty or something. Who gives you the right to judge? Speaking in tongues is a gift from God. It is the Holy Spirit providing words for people to speak when they can't think of adequate words of their own to praise God, to ask for the welfare of another, or simply to express their joy that Christ loves them. It's beautiful."

I looked at her as if she were somebody else. What had they done to her? "Two months ago you didn't believe in this either. What's changed?"

"Two months ago I didn't know what I believed. All I knew was there must be something more to being a Christian than what I knew. God didn't seem real enough or close enough. There was no joy in me like the Bible describes. Well, there is real joy in our group, Bob. The Holy Spirit is there; you can just feel Him! These are real, alive, turned-on Christians! I wish you could see it for yourself. I learned that it is the Holy Spirit who makes the difference. It's all right in the Bible, but I hadn't paid attention before. Speaking in tongues is one of the gifts of the Holy Spirit. He gave it to *me!* And Bob, I'd never felt the reality of God so keenly until after I had received this gift."

Outside, a car raced its motor as it passed our house, but soon the Saturday-morning stillness was restored. "Can you hear yourself speaking when you are praying in tongues?"

"Of course."

"Can you understand any of the words?"

"No, but that's not important. God understands them. It's some language, though, because I've studied languages enough to know. It has rhythm, inflection, and punctuation. And sometimes it changes from one language into another. You can hear it change."

I squeezed my hands together until the knuckles whitened. "Do you have any control over it? I mean—can you do it or not do it anytime you want?"

"Yes, of course!" Now she smiled. "You can pray in tongues anytime and anywhere. You can pray as loudly or as softly as you like, even to yourself. You can even sing in tongues, and sometimes someone does in our group meeting and it is perfectly lovely! You'd think so too if you heard it." She paused. "You know, this is beginning to sound like a cross-examination."

"Barbara, I'm simply trying to understand this thing!" I exploded. My stomach was knotted again and I felt terribly threatened for some reason. "I don't think this is a gift from God at all. No sir!"

Her smile vanished. "Well, what do you think we're doing, just making it up?"

"Maybe, I don't know. Maybe some are just making it up. Maybe some are kind of getting hypnotized into doing it through the group influence with all the singing and clapping. But there are all kinds of spirits, you know that. I think this could be dangerous."

"You mean," she snapped, "that it may come from the devil?"

"It's possible."

"Well, you're wrong, Bob, and I resent your implications. If you heard someone speaking in tongues, you'd know they couldn't possibly make it up. You can tell if someone tries. And group hypnotism is ridiculous; several people have received the gift in the privacy of their own homes with no one else present. Celia did, and Betty who lives up the street. How do you explain that?" She glared at me a moment before continuing. "Read Acts again. Read about Pentecost and how the disciples received the gift of tongues. Read 1 Corinthians. Paul says he spoke in tongues more than them all and that he wished *all* of them would speak in tongues." Anger was definitely in her voice now. "Are *you* going to say Saint Paul was wrong and that *you* are right? Are you calling Paul a liar?"

Her rising tone had hardened my face into an unchanging scowl. "Read James," I slapped back. "He says the tongue should be the most feared member of the body, that the tongue is a restless evil, full of poison. Are *you* going to call Saint James a liar?"

"Oh, I don't care what you say! I know my gift is from God whether you want to believe it or not! You can't know what I feel! You don't know everything!"

If we hadn't had other disagreements in the past, our discussion would probably have ended right there in the storm of her last comment. Fortunately, we had learned a simple little trick that punches holes in the communication barriers that anger erects. I got up now and refilled the coffee cups. We both recognized this as a pulling back and regrouping sort of action, so neither spoke. With relief I noted the kids were absorbed in their cartoons, oblivious to the bedroom war. Regrettably, they were not to remain uninvolved for long.

We drank our coffee in silence for a time, each lost in his or her own thoughts. Though the anger had receded, tension still filled the room like summer humidity.

Barbara was the first to speak again. "I *knew* this would happen. They told me the devil would very quickly try to make me doubt my experience. It's happening."

"And I, I suppose, am the devil?" My voice was flat with the misery that thought gave to me.

"No, but he's using you, can't you see that? He wants to make me draw back from God, to give up my gift, and he's attacking me through my marriage. He *knows* how important that is to me!"

"Do you mean that to even *question* this experience is the work of the devil?"

"I know the Bible says to test the spirits. But it also says you can quench the Spirit by disbelief!"

I studied her face a moment. There was actually some fear in it. Here was an obstacle I hadn't anticipated. Apparently, she had been told that any questioning would place her in danger of losing the Holy Spirit. She must defend Baptism in the Holy Spirit and speaking in tongues against all argument, by blind faith if need be, or risk angering God. I had to know more about this group that now seemed to exercise such great control over my wife's thinking. Just what had happened, anyway?

"Barb, just what goes on in this group of yours? We've always discussed things before, but now you're accusing me of devil possession to even talk about this subject."

Her mood quickly changed back to anger. "Didn't you do the same to me a minute ago? Nothing 'goes on'! You'd like to picture them as something sinister, wouldn't you? Well, they're not witches or hobgoblins or whatever else is going through your mind. They're the sweetest, happiest, most dedicated group of Christian women I've ever known. They showed me love, nothing else. They accepted me just as I was. They've shown me how the Holy Spirit can fill persons with joy and give them power to witness freely for Jesus Christ and to heal the sick. They *care* about other people enough to pray specifically for the solution to their problems. They introduced *me* to the Holy Spirit, Bob, and now that I know what Christian joy is, I won't give it up!"

Though she was talking about the joy of the Holy Spirit in her words, I had the distinct impression she was really talking about the *group*. I persisted, *"How* did they introduce you to the Holy Spirit?"

She raised an eyebrow. "Do you really want to know, or are you just looking for ways to persecute them?"

"I really want to know."

"All right. We had been having group prayer and I was crying. Before you say anything, let me explain that I frequently cried at the meetings. It's all so moving, praising God that way and experiencing genuine concern for others. Anyway, that day Celia noticed me crying. She came over and said 'I believe Barbara would like to be baptized in the Holy Spirit.' I nodded my assent."

"Did you tell her you wanted to speak in tongues?" I broke in.

"No. I just wanted to have the Holy Spirit like the others had Him."

"Then what happened?"

"Well, don't interrupt! They took me into a back bedroom and we all prayed together, asking for the Baptism in the Holy Spirit. After awhile, it happened. It's hard to explain just *what* happened. I felt funny. It was as if I had split into two people, with the one me watching what the other me was doing. Then these words started pouring out of my throat, words I'd never heard before. I didn't make them up, Bob, I couldn't have. They came out without any effort on my own part. I could hear them, but they weren't mine. They belonged to the Holy Spirit; they were His gift to me!"

It was a few seconds before I could speak again. I felt a little dizzy. "How many were in the room with you?"

"Five or six, I don't remember exactly."

"In Sherrill's book, when describing his own experience, the people gathered all around him, I got the impression they even put their hands on him, and they prayed in tongues. Is that what your group did?"

She hesitated briefly, then said, "Yes, some did."

"Did they ask that you be given the gift of tongues, even though you didn't ask for it?"

Another hesitation. "Yes, but I wanted it. Even if I didn't tell them, I wanted it. I could have objected, but I didn't."

The scene was alive in my mind now—Barbara crying in emotional boil-over, a group of women she respected steering her into a back room, the group gathering around her, telling her to pray, holding many hands upon her body, surrounding her with the sounds of tongues, asking the same phenomenon for her, wanting her to speak in tongues, too. My vision blurred with uncontrolled anger. Like Jesus on the porch of the temple, I wanted to wade through that group with a whip!

"They had no right! Who do they think they are, praying for something you hadn't asked for? Why couldn't they content themselves by simply asking that the Holy Spirit come to you?"

"I wanted it, Bob, and they sensed it." After another moment, she added, "There's nothing wrong with it. It's in the Bible!"

Boiling over with frustration and indignation, I grabbed the coffee cups for another refill. "I know! I know! You keep telling me that! But I want to read those parts of the Bible again!"

Sure enough, it is in the Bible. Barbara made up the bed as I read the story of Pentecost in Acts 2 and Paul's instructions in 1 Corinthians, chapters 12–14. But what Barbara had seen, or had been led to see, as clear instructions to desire to speak in tongues, I saw entirely differently.

Finally I looked up and pronounced bluntly, "Paul is doing everything in his power to discourage speaking in tongues short of absolutely forbidding them. How can people read this and get anything else out of it?

"Doesn't Paul list speaking in tongues as one of the gifts of the Holy Spirit?"

"Yes, in next to last place!"

"But it *is* one of the gifts."

"Yes, but. . . ."

"Doesn't Paul also say that he wished all of them

spoke in tongues?" Barbara's eyes blazed as she took up the challenge in my voice.

"He follows that one immediately by saying he'd *rather* have them prophesy. And he also says that in church he would rather speak five words with understanding than *ten thousand* words in an unknown tongue!"

"In *church,* yes. But he also says tongues are for self-edification. Our group insists that praying in tongues is mainly for private worship. And don't diminish the importance of building up one's self, especially in this day and age."

"Since you seem to believe literally every word Paul says," I said sarcastically, "how about this instruction that women shouldn't speak in church? How about *this* instruction, that they should *ask their husbands at home about spiritual questions?*"

"That," she almost shouted at me, "is an allusion to the customs of the times, and you know it!"

"Oh, I see," I said in my best courtroom voice. "We are to take *this* verse literally and toss *that* one out as it suits our purpose! How very convenient!"

I could literally *feel* her projection of hostility, but she remained silent.

"Well, let's leave that for the moment and go to Acts," I continued. "Here the disciples received the Holy Spirit and started speaking in tongues, but there is a major difference between what they did and what you and your group seem to be doing. At Pentecost, everyone present *understood* what was said, each in his own language. How do you explain that?"

"Paul says there are tongues of men and tongues of angels. God chose to give the disciples the tongues of men on that day. Many people have spoken in known foreign languages since then, too. Don't you remember that from Sherrill's book?"

"I remember second- and third-hand accounts, yes. But I must doubt them since Sherrill wrote his book *after* he started believing in the doctrine himself. He must have been very eager to believe those stories."

"Oh Bob!" She looked at me as if I'd just taken another prod from the devil.

I took another tack. "Okay, whenever I find something in the epistles that seems out of place, I check it against what Jesus said. Did Jesus ever advocate speaking in tongues?"

"Yes. Mark 16:17," she quickly shot back.

Surprised, I leafed through my Revised Standard Version. There it was, along with other signs that would identify Jesus' followers. But it was in footnote! "C'mon, Barbara! Even the Bible scholars can't agree that this passage is even a valid part of Scripture!"

"Some theologians even say that God is dead. That should tell us a lot about what theologians know."

"How about these other signs mentioned in Mark then? Does your group advocate picking up snakes or taking poisons? Would *you* pick up a snake right now to prove your faith?" I knew, of course, that Barb had always had a fear of snakes, bugs—any crawly thing. "Or is this, too, conveniently ignored?" My voice crackled with indignation.

She started to speak, but closed her mouth again until her trembling subsided. When she did speak, it was in low, measured tones. "You can think me stupid if you like, Bob, but you can't convince me my experience wasn't both real and from God. You're not me; you can't judge what I felt. You can't judge these other women either. In you, I see anger and hate and prejudice, and not so very long ago, defeatism. In them, I see love and joy and hope and compassion. I have seen people healed by power going out from the Holy Spirit dwelling in them. I've felt His presence in me. All your words, no matter how cleverly put, can't change what I've felt and seen. I won't drag you to any Pentecostal meetings, I won't speak in tongues in front of you, and I won't have any group meetings at our house. But I won't quit the group or give up my gift, and you'll just have to accept that."

It sounded good, this suppression of logic by experience. It had an appeal even for me. I had to remind myself that experiences can be misleading. How many times as an engineer had I probed an apparent fact, only to find the real truth hidden somewhere behind the illusion? No, I couldn't give up the logical probing. Truth would stand when it was finally reached.

So our argument continued, but much of it was just a rehash of what had already been said. Somewhere along the way, I asked two more stupid questions. More than once, Barbara had commented on the coldness of the institutional church. On one such occasion, I asked bluntly, "Can you still go to *our* church and participate in the services?"

"Of course I can. Don't be silly! I just wish we could liven it up a little and take the formal chill out of the air. I wish it could be more like the early Christian church."

At another point I asked, "Can you still pray in English and feel it means anything?"

She looked at me as if I were crazy. "Certainly! You know what your trouble is, Bob? You're ignorant on this subject. You don't know what you're trying to talk about."

Oh, that stung! But it was true. Barbara had already read several books loaned to her by her group members. I had read only the book by Sherrill. I tucked away a mental note—educate yourself!

By lunchtime, however, it seemed we had reached a reluctant compromise. Neither had changed the other's mind one whit, but it appeared an arrangement of tolerance had been made. We even laughed a little at ourselves for our previous intensity. The truce was not to remain intact for long, however.

Barbara mentioned something about teaching Sunday school together the coming church year. Except for the last several months when we were getting established in our new house, we had worked with junior-high youth both in Sunday school and in prayer groups for the past three years. We had been a team.

"You can teach a class if you like, but we obviously can't teach together anymore," I retorted with a rueful little laugh.

She looked stricken. This was a development she hadn't expected. "Why not?"

"Simple. We don't believe the same things anymore, so how can we possibly teach together?"

"Why, I don't see what difference that should make."

"It makes all the difference in the world. You now believe in Baptism in the Holy Spirit as an experience subsequent to conversion, and in speaking in tongues. I don't. Since you believe in it, you will naturally want to teach it. As soon as you do, however, I will contradict you. So there we will be, arguing in front of the kids. And we're supposed to be the experts. It just wouldn't work, Barbara."

She disagreed, and the wound of division was reopened as we fussed, as it would be often in the future. This time Jerry and Judy were present and they winced as each verbal blow landed. Who can measure what harm we did? Finally, it was ended, not from agreement but from emotional exhaustion and from necessity. Some jobs *had* to be done that weekend, even if there were no time left for any fun things.

All that afternoon and evening I was eaten up by worry. If the prayer group could talk Barbara into speaking in tongues, what else could it influence her to do? I was convinced she had yielded herself not only to God, but to this human group as well. What demands would it make? What experiences would it seek? Barbara was right in thinking I saw the group as sinister. I imagined a giant tug-of-war with Barbara serving as the rope. I was so dangerously close to the line before I even knew a contest was in progress!

Sunday morning, May 7, we skipped Sunday school. I didn't want to be drawn into an argument with a whole platoon of tongue speakers! Not yet, anyway. We did attend worship services, however. My eyes scanned the congregation as the processional was being played, but I saw very few of those I now knew spoke in tongues.

As we sang the hymns, I noticed that Barbara remained silent. And as our minister presented the sermon, she fidgeted nervously. Two weeks before, over one hundred people had joined our church on the same Sunday morning. It had been a tremendous sight to see that many people at the altar at one time. Nevertheless, when Reverend Fellows deviated from his text and referred to that event this morning, Barbara flinched and even scowled. It was hard to keep my mind on the sermon, knowing she was disapproving of something.

Just before we reached Reverend Fellows at the door in the handshake line, another layman complimented his sermon. "Thank you very much," he boomed loud enough for us to hear. "You know, I usually try to prepare my sermons at least a year in advance, but I just had to make special comment today on so many people joining the church together. Wasn't that wonderful?" I saw Barbara flinch again.

When we arrived home, she nervously moved about putting things down a little harder than usual and closing doors a little faster than usual. This was a sure sign she had something on her mind she wanted to say.

Sighing, I sat down at the desk again and said, "Okay, what is it?"

Immediately she broke into tears. "How could he prepare his sermons a *year* ahead of time and give any heed to what Jesus wants him to say? Why can't he just get up there and preach whatever the Holy Spirit gives him to say on Sunday morning?"

"Barb, you surely don't believe that Reverend Fellows doesn't have the Holy Spirit? Do you?" She cried softly, not answering. "Barb, I'm sure he prays for guidance on his sermons when he prepares them, no matter when he intends to use them. If he didn't listen to the Holy Spirit, would he have departed from his text today?"

"For what?" she sobbed. "To brag on those new church members? Well, it takes more than belonging to a church to be a Christian, let me tell you!"

"That's true, of course. But a church is for seekers as well as believers. Jesus didn't shut out everyone except his own disciples. And Barb, let me tell you that your prayer group has no monopoly on the Holy Spirit!"

That did it. We were off and running on another argument-discussion. Nothing had changed; the same ground was covered, only a little more forcibly this time. We approached the question from dozens of different directions. We stretched it, bent it, kicked it, and spun it around within the limits of our knowledge. We wet it with tears. In the end, we had the same reluctant compromise. We also agreed we were through talking about tongues forever, just as I had requested.

Forever, it turned out, lasted only four hours and I

was the treaty breaker. That evening, the combined choirs of our church gave a spring concert and we had promised some teen-age participants to be present. The music was excellent and I was thrilled by it. Afterwards, I rushed around to different choir members offering congratulations. The buoyancy persisted as we got into our car to go home. "Now *that* to me is the language of *Angels!*" I pompously declared. Barbara stiffened as if she had been slapped. To be perfectly honest, I guess I had meant it to be just that. Retaliation would come.

4

A Basis for Dissent

A definite chill gripped the Branch household on Monday morning. Barbara and I said not two words to one another over breakfast and my departure was ignored. Bitterness generated over the weekend hung heavily in the air. Without formulating the thoughts in my mind, I instinctively knew we couldn't just drop this subject as I'd requested. No marriage could survive this kind of freeze.

I'd never felt so tired before! Emotional upheaval extracts more from the body than a day of manual labor. Yet, sleep had been elusive. Dark thoughts had churned through my mind until the wee hours, keeping me in worried wakefulness. Now as I steered the pickup through a familiar traffic pattern the thoughts resumed, as if my mind had the benefit of some kind of supercharger that was denied to my body.

None of my arguments had had any visible effect on Barbara. It was as if she had erected a force shield against all dissent. She was so *sure* of her new beliefs, and she was reassured and reinforced by legions of local believers. For two months they had imbued her with their theology, surrounded their doctrine with spiritual glamour, and finally had sold her the entire package. Then they planted the idea that any dissent might be evil. Against all this careful preparation I had been able only to advance the opinions of one person, myself, a person without credentials, especially to my own wife who knew all my frailties.

It was obvious that it would take allies and indisputable facts to penetrate this defensive screen. There *must* be others with greater wisdom than I who disputed the claims of the Pentecostals! Maybe Barbara would at least listen to *them*. But who were they? Certainly my wife's friends hadn't loaned her any books which *questioned* the Movement—quite the contrary! That would be *my* job—to seek out authorities and authors who disagreed with Pentecostalism, to find local people who opposed the Movement, to find scriptural flaws in the doctrine—in short, to establish a credible basis for dissent.

There was the possibility, of course, that I would find *no* flaws and *no* allies. As an engineer I knew I would have to accept that truth too, if I found it, no matter how repugnant it was to me personally. But also as an engineer, I knew I couldn't accept a whole new doctrine without a thorough investigation—particularly *this* doctrine.

The traffic thickened as I neared the factory. Slanting rays of morning sunlight reflected off dust specks on the windshield, creating a glare that made me squint and ease off on the accelerator. There would be little sense in adding an accident to my other troubles! Finally, a traffic signal stopped my progress altogether and I was forced to sit and wait.

What was the red light that kept me from accepting this new doctrine prima facie? Aside from my early exposure to Pentecostals, there were two things in particular and they both stemmed from Sherrill's book. One was his graphic description of his own Baptism in the Holy Spirit. Step by step he had described this experience—what had happened, what he had seen, what he had felt. With one notable exception, I had experienced the *very same things* in my own *conversion* experience! The exception was the phenomenon of speaking in unknown tongues. In my experience, however, no one had mentioned speaking in tongues beforehand, no one had glamorized and prepared me to do it, no hands were laid on, and no one had demonstrated it in my presence. Yet I received the Holy Spirit just as surely as John Sherrill did! The tongues, I concluded, were just something extraneous tacked on to a genuine spiritual experience.

Secondly, I remembered his description of Charles Parham's original group at Stone's Folly. There was nothing to indicate this group practiced the excesses exhibited by the religious students in my hometown; yet this group as well as several other Pentecostal denominations were reported to have their origins in Parham's group. What change had occurred over the years? Was it possible that the phenomenon of speaking in tongues started a demonstrative process that demanded stronger and wilder expression the more it was practiced? Did a tongue speaker gradually lose control of the experience as he sought an ever-increasing spiritual awareness?

I strongly suspected the last two statements were true and it alarmed me. Barbara was so proud of the control she exercised over the phenomenon now. Two years from now, would she still be its master? Or would she then be led to run senselessly down the street in the middle of the night? Would she have incidents of semi-paralyzed twitching collapses? Would she howl and moan and stutter at church services? I couldn't abandon my wife to such a possibility if there were any chance of and basis for preventing it!

The light changed and I jerked my pickup around a corner so fast the rear tires squealed. Oh, how I resented the members of that prayer group! If they wanted to play with fire, let them, but they had no right to seduce my wife into such a dangerous game!

Work was the last thing on my mind as I arrived at my desk. Without hesitation, I grabbed the phone book and looked up Murray Simms's extension. Seconds later he was on the line.

"Murray, I need to talk to you about this speaking-in-tongues business. Remember how interested everyone at the retreat was in that subject? Well I am too, now, but in a different way and I need your help."

"What can I do for you?" he replied cautiously.

"I want to discuss the whole matter with you. But before I do, I need to do some reading. Only I don't know what to read. Do you have any books which *oppose* speaking in tongues?"

He thought a minute. "No, I don't think so, but I do have an article by a Christian professor of anthropology. He made a study of how the phenomenon has appeared in different ethnological groups around the world. It's quite scholarly, but he makes some interesting points. Would you like me to make a copy of it and send it to you?"

"By all means. I'm interested in anything I can get my hands on."

"I think there's a bibliography at the end of the article that might help you. A lot of books are available, both pro and con, but I can't think of any titles offhand which take the opposing view. Tell you what. Go down to the Christian Supply Center and ask for Arnie Samuelson. He could guide you right to several."

"Arnie . . . Samuelson?" I questioned, making notes as fast as I could.

"That's right. He's the owner and he's helped me often in the past." He paused. "Do you have a problem, Bob?"

"Yeah, I sure do, and that's what I'd like to talk to you about. Will you have any time near the end of the week, after I've had a chance to read?"

I could hear him flipping calendar pages. Murray was a supervisor as well as an engineer. He worked with Young Life and was very much in demand as a Christian speaker. I'd be lucky if he found an open slot. But I had a special reason for wanting to talk to him.

"How about . . . Thursday afternoon about four-thirty? I could stay a little while after working hours if necessary."

"Great, I'll come over to your office. Thanks a million, Murray!"

The next hour was eaten up by duties, but as soon as some slack appeared, I grabbed my coat and charged out. It didn't occur to me to check with anybody; I just left. Soon my pickup was parked in front of the Christian Supply Center.

"Arnie Samuelson?" a woman clerk responded to my query. "No, he's out of town until Wednesday on a buying trip. Could I help you?"

"Possibly. I'm looking for some books on the Charismatic Movement which take an opposing view to speaking in tongues. Do you have any?"

A cloud passed over the woman's face and a look of incredulity appeared. It was a look I would see repeated often by others in the next several weeks. "No, I don't think we have. But you're welcome to browse if you'd like."

She guided me to a particular section of the store and I was stunned by the number of books displayed. Many of the covers were illustrated with descending doves and with flames of fire. The titles were liberally sprinkled with words and phrases such as "Pentecost," "Baptism in the Holy Spirit," "Speaking in Tongues," "Joy," and the like. There were books on healing and on recognizing the spirits and on casting out demons. It was overwhelming. I backed out of the store empty-handed, muttering something about returning later.

Clearly, the Pentecostals were way out in front of me! I retreated to the factory and began a desk-drumming vigil of the incoming mailbox.

The article arrived that afternoon and I lost no time in reading it. It was written by George J. Jennings, an anthropology professor at Wheaton College, and was entitled "An Ethnological Study of Glossolalia." I was soon to learn that *glossolalia* was another way of saying *speaking in tongues*. As Murray had said, the article *was* quite scholarly, having been written for publication in the *Journal of the American Scientific Affiliation,* and I had to back up several times to fully absorb the professor's meaning. Still, it was the first material I'd seen that expressed doubt that God was the origin of the phenomenon, so I worked eagerly over it.

Professor Jennings pointed out that three explanations are often offered for the occurrence of glossolalia: (1) it is inspired by the devil; (2) it is inspired by God; or, (3) it is a psychological phenomenon with no spiritual inspiration at all, either good or bad. The first explanation he rejected quite quickly for very much the same reasons Barbara had given me over the weekend. He expressed great doubt the second was true because of the use of glossolalia by widely dispersed non-Christian cultures over the centuries and today. Because of this, and because there were some striking similarities between Pentecostal meetings and glossolalic non-Christian ceremonies, he concluded the psychological explanation was true.

This was the very kind of information I needed! The trouble with the article, though, was that I'd never get Barbara to wrestle with the style as I had. I needed the same information presented clearly and forcefully, à la John Sherrill. Fortunately, a bibliography was provided and I underlined several titles to investigate.

The article also provided me with another question for Barbara. Professor Jennings indicated that it was not uncommon for a novitiate to be asked to repeat a key word or phrase over and over, when seeking the Baptism in the Holy Spirit, to stimulate the onset of tongues. The example given was "Jesus! Jesus! Jesus!" Was this true? Had Barbara been told to do this? And if so, what kind of spiritual gift had to be stimulated by a physical action?

I didn't feel quite so isolated in my opinions that evening, but I didn't discuss it with Barbara either. There was much to be done yet. I didn't want to go back on the firing line with only one more bullet!

I chafed under my duties on Tuesday morning until I could once more break away. Back at the Christian Supply Center, I searched the shelves for the titles I had jotted down from Professor Jennings's bibliography. This time I scored, and quickly bought two books written by Anthony A. Hoekema, a professor of systematic theology at Calvin Theological Seminary. One was *What About Tongue-Speaking?* and the other was *Holy Spirit Baptism.* The same saleslady took my money and made change without a smile or comment.

Time was stolen from my job to read these books, I am now ashamed to admit. I was like a man possessed; my mind refused to concentrate on drawings or calculations or reports. A sense of danger gripped me, focusing all my energies and capacities on the problem that threatened. It took Tuesday afternoon and Wednesday

morning to read the two books, which was remarkable
speed for a normally slow reader. When I finished, I
knew I had something.

Hoekema approached the issue of speaking in
tongues theologically and he wrote with a style much
easier to read. One by one he discussed the pillars of
Pentecostal doctrine and one by one he gave his reasons for disagreeing with it. Verse by verse he exam-
ined the language of the early manuscripts to establish
not only the meaning but the intent. In the end he
concluded that Baptism in the Holy Spirit as a necessary experience subsequent to conversion did *not* have
valid scriptural basis. And though he would not say
that praying in unknown tongues was worthless, he
expressed serious doubts that it could hold very much
spiritual value when the speaker didn't even know
what he was saying.

The latter feeling was perfectly compatible with my
concept that God makes perfect sense. Daily I work
with the physical laws of Creation. With infinite
genius, God established an exceedingly complex uni-
verse with marvelous interconnections and interde-
pendencies that fit together in perfect harmony. He did
the same with the human body. Amidst all this logical
order, would He then introduce nonsense? I'd found
another ally.

Momentum would not let me sit still during the
lunch hour. I went back to the bookstore only to find
that Arnie was having *his* lunch. I browsed the shelves
that were now becoming more familiar and scored
again. This time, by reading prefaces and scanning

pages, I was able to isolate Donald Burdick's *Tongues: To Speak or Not to Speak,* and John Kildahl's *The Psychology of Speaking in Tongues.* The former is a professor at Conservative Baptist Theological Seminary; the latter, a psychotherapist in charge of pastoral psychology studies at New York Theological Seminary. I read Burdick's book that afternoon and his arguments closely paralleled those of Hoekema, except that *he* was convinced that the true gift of tongues had passed out of the church with the Apostles. Kildahl's book was longer and so I set it aside for later.

The chill was still on at home. Dinner was mostly silent except for Jerry's and Judy's chatter; Barbara and I politely listened. We didn't go to the Bible-study meeting; in fact, we didn't even mention it. This was a prudent action by Barbara since I now knew that most of the women who would be present were tongue speakers who were also members of her prayer group. By now I considered the Bible-study group as little more than a front organization for the Charismatic Movement, dedicated to the promotion of speaking in tongues. It was no coincidence, I was convinced, that we were studying the Book of Mark, the only Gospel with a reference to tongues.

If I accomplished any productive work on Thursday, I can't remember what it was. My thoughts were occupied wholly by what I'd read and by what I was going to say to Murray. When 4:30 finally arrived, I hurried over to his office. Since he was a supervisor, we had the benefit of privacy.

"Murray, I'll come right to the point. Barbara has started speaking in tongues and I don't believe in them. No, more than that, I guess you could say I'm very strongly prejudiced against them." I then told him why as briefly as I could. "At the retreat, if I remember correctly, you indicated that *your* wife spoke in tongues but that you didn't. Is that right?"

His gaze never wavered from mine. "Yes, that's correct."

"Well, how do you guys work it out? I think Barbara and I are in for trouble."

"In the first place, Bob, I don't feel about tongues the way you do. To me, they are not—what shall I say— dangerous? I think of them as a phenomenon which helps some people in their spiritual lives. We could argue back and forth about their origin, whether they are from God or whether it is a psychological trick, but I don't intend to do that. The important thing to me is, what is their effect on a given individual? Do they help or hurt? Linda had an insecure childhood and an overdeveloped inferiority complex. When she started speaking in tongues, believing them to be a gift from God, her personality improved markedly. She gained confidence in herself, she was able to show more affection for others, and her work for Christ took on new energy and purpose. In short, the fruits were good, and '. . . you will know them by their fruits.' Now, what is the case with Barbara?"

I raised my eyebrows and sighed. "I'll have to admit that it seems to have had a positive effect on her, too.

She has been more loving, more self-assured and enthusiastic. But it's all based on a counterfeit miracle, Murray, and that's not right!"

He smiled tolerantly. "Can you prove that?"

"Not yet," I admitted.

"Bob, if speaking in tongues is helping Barbara, why should you object to it?"

"I'm scared to death of what it might lead to. What are the long-term effects? Who knows?"

"I don't think there *are* any bad effects. Oh, I suppose some individuals abuse the experience and use it as an excuse for emotional extremism. But in my work with teen-agers, the usual pattern is initial enthusiasm followed by a gradually decreasing use of tongues. This has been Linda's pattern also; the only time she prays in tongues now is during her private devotional at home."

"Do you believe in Baptism in the Holy Spirit, Murray?"

He collected his thoughts for a moment. "I believe the Holy Spirit is received during a true conversion. There are periods thereafter when a person is 'filled' for some special work or crisis, but he doesn't go through a period of limbo awaiting the arrival of the Holy Spirit once he accepts Christ as Lord and Saviour."

"Then you think that speaking in tongues is *not* a necessary evidence of the Holy Spirit's presence as the Pentecostals claim?"

"That's right." He smiled at me again. "But I'm not

going to say that speaking in tongues is not the work of the Holy Spirit either. You're blowing this one phenomenon up too big in your mind, Bob. I suppose this is understandable because of your background. But I would recommend that you not oppose it. If it is helping Barbara, be glad for it and trust God that everything will turn out all right."

"I don't know if I can do that, Murray, but I appreciate your talking to me. Hey, it's 5:30! I've got to run!"

"Keep in touch," I heard him say as I left the office. I had to sprint to my gate before it was locked for the evening.

Frankly, I was disappointed by the interview. Murray would have been a powerful ally had he taken a strong stand against tongue speaking. He had spoken often at our church, even though he maintained a membership elsewhere. Hoekema had recommended tolerance also, at the close of his books, even as Murray had. Every time I thought of tolerance, however, the image of that young man hurtling down the street superimposed itself on my mind. Murray and Hoekema hadn't seen that boy; Bob Branch had!

About once every seven years, our factory has an open house for employees' families. Saturday, May 13, was scheduled for this rare event. I'd been eager for Jerry and Judy to see where their daddy worked, especially since I couldn't take them in at any other time. I had to postpone my reading program that Friday to help dress up our area and to prepare displays. Thousands were expected; we didn't want to look sloppy, particularly since it would take another seven years to live down a bad impression. By the end of the day, the plant looked its Sunday best.

Dinner that evening followed its usual strained pattern. I picked at my food without real appetite. When I left the table my trousers were noticeably sagging, so I went to the bathroom and mounted the scales. I could hardly believe my eyes! I had lost eight pounds without trying! For a guy who had to work at controlling his weight, such a loss would have normally required four weeks. I got off and on the scales several times, but the result was always the same. Eight pounds!

It was still early so I picked up John Kildahl's book and started reading. My intention was to read leisurely, but before the first page was finished I was already bearing down with the same urgent intensity I had brought to the other books.

Kildahl's approach was clinical in nature, though it also presented a history of tongue speaking down through the ages. His book was really a report of ten years of research on the subject, funded originally by the Lutheran church and later by the National Institute of Mental Health. He had traveled twice from coast to coast attending Pentecostal meetings and interviewing tongue speakers. In plain language he explained his results and gave his conclusions.

Like a bandit filling his bandolier, I latched onto bullet after bullet I could fire at Barbara and any other tongue speaker. Kildahl verified Professor Jennings's claim that the onset of tongues was commonly stimulated by the repetition of key words and phrases. In addition to this, he observed that a human leader usually played an important role in the Baptism in the Holy Spirit. The leader was someone the novitiate respected and admired, someone he or she could place perfect trust in, much as a subject of hypnotism trusts the hypnotist.

I paused here and thought back over the weeks. Yes, there had been a woman Barbara had mentioned several times, a woman I'd never met who with her husband had been in town for only a few weeks before moving on to operate a permanent Christian retreat. They had sold all their possessions to enter this work and Barbara had been tremendously impressed. "Their original ambitions and goals remind me so much of our own," she had said one day, "and to think they've given it all up for full-time Christian work!" Had this woman been Barbara's leader?

Kildahl's tests revealed that tongue speakers were no more or no less mentally healthy than non-tongue speakers, but that they did tend to be more dependent. He noted that tongue speakers were usually very defensive and often felt they were persecuted, a condition which made them draw together in close-knit groups. Certainly Barbara had exhibited this characteristic. In the end, Kildahl expressed his opinion that speaking in tongues was a psychological phenomenon in which the subconscious mind controlled the speech organs. It was induced in a manner not the same as, but similar to, hypnotism. It was not a gift at all, but a human experience that was *taught*.

This was what I needed! Facts. Examples. Comparisons. But anyone who fools with ordnance knows that there is always the risk that the high explosive will unexpectedly go off in your face. Not all of Kildahl's observations fit neatly into my preprepared mold.

For instance, he also observed that a tongue speaker's experience seemed as vital, if not more so, to the speaker a year later, and he had noted no loss of control. Also, the experience seemed to have *beneficial* effects for the speaker in terms of personality integration. This confirmed what Murray and I had seen in our wives.

The biggest explosion, however, was Kildahl's observation that in 85 percent of the case histories, a crisis situation existed in the novitiate's life immediately before he began speaking in tongues. One of the crisis situations mentioned was a marriage that seemed on the verge of collapse. I thought back over the days of my severe depression over the lost money, days in which I would sit staring at the wall oblivious to activities around me, inattentive to Barbara or the children, unresponsive to their efforts to cheer me up. They needed the love I withheld. The conclusion was as disturbing as it was inescapable—I had unwittingly *driven* Barbara into her experience!

Luckily my teeth survived the scourging they received from the brush that evening as I angrily prepared for bed. How easy I had made it for the tongue speakers to capture my wife! They couldn't have designed a better preparation. Well, things wouldn't be so easy from here on out—Bob Branch was on the counterattack!

5

So Much for Family Day

Saturday, May 13, came in with its dander up. By 6 A.M. I was standing at the kitchen window looking at the dark skies. Brawny thunderheads pushed and shoved one another around the tops of our mountains, completely obscuring the peaks. At lower levels, lighter colored mists rose from the arroyos, giving the appearance of freshly healed scars on a craggy face. Not to be outdone in this show of force, an arrogant wind gustily slapped the landscape, bending trees first to the west and then to the north. At a glance one would have thought that Family Day was in jeopardy.

"Bluff, pure bluff," I thought derisively as I took another sip of coffee and watched a truant wrapping paper fly by in panic. Man must have learned that game from Nature. We only received eight inches of rainfall each year, most of it coming during a two-month season, and this was *not* the time for it. In a couple of hours the sun would most likely be shining and this sham storm would be in full retreat.

I broke away from the meteorologic melodrama long

enough to move the TV into the children's bedroom. Perhaps the cartoons would drown out Barbara's and my voices if things didn't go well. As added insurance, I closed their door behind me as I left. There seemed no sense in involving them in a subject they couldn't yet comprehend.

I was finishing my third cup of coffee when Barbara entered the kitchen. Fatigue showed on her face. Obviously she wasn't sleeping well either.

"Barb, I want to talk."

She didn't look at me but moved instead directly to the percolator. As the brown liquid sloshed into her cup, she answered flatly, "Oh? What about?"

"About this speaking-in-tongues business."

She eased onto a barstool, still avoiding my gaze. "Sorry, I can't do that. My husband said he didn't want to hear any more about that subject in this house."

"Okay, so I said that, but I've had to change my mind. This subject is too big to ignore."

"Oh, that's just ducky; you've changed your mind. *Well, I haven't!*"

"Barb. . . ."

"No! There's nothing more to say. Do you think I *like* being insulted, being made to feel guilty? *'That* to me is the language of angels,' you said. I haven't done anything wrong and I don't have to listen to your jibes, Bob!"

"For Pete's sake, I. . . . Look, I've been reading some books and I've come across some new information I think we ought to discuss. The least you could do. . . . Barb! Where are you going?"

She had hurriedly picked up her cup and was moving quickly toward our bedroom. "No!" she threw back over her shoulder.

I scrambled to my feet and followed her. "Barb, you come back here! Barb!"

I was passing the children's bedroom when the door opened and Jerry poked his blond head out into the hallway. "Daddy? Is something wrong?"

Only a stone man could have ignored the look of fear on his son's face. For a moment I let the anger tremble through and out of me; then I put my hand on Jerry's shoulder and guided him back into his room. Judy sat on the bed in her granny gown, worried, completely ignoring the cavorting cartoon figures on the TV screen.

"Kids. . . ." I ran a hand through my hair and rubbed the back of my neck as I fumbled for the right words. "Kids, your mother and I are having . . . a disagreement about something you wouldn't understand. We'll work it out, don't you worry about it, but it's going to take a little time. You can help us by staying in your room this morning and giving us a chance to talk together. Tell you what, if you can be that grown-up, we'll try our best not to fuss at each other. Okay?"

They agreed but still looked worried as I eased out of the room. I retreated into the den for awhile to regain my composure. We *must* settle this, I thought, before the kids get hurt by it.

Finally, I got up and joined Barbara in our bedroom. She was face down upon the bed and crying softly.

"Did you hear that?"

"Yes. Bob, we have to stop this fighting! Jerry and Judy will be scared to death. It's not right."

"I agree, but we can't just drop it where we are now, either. We didn't have a marriage this past week, Barb. It was more like two travelers snowed in and forced to share the same accommodations."

"And whose fault was that?"

I pushed my hand through my hair again and lowered my head. "Mine, I guess, and I apologize."

"Well, thank you for that much anyway."

"Barb, let's start this day all over again. We have to talk this thing out, but let's do it without all the excitement, without shouting at one another. How about it?"

She kneaded one hand with the other. "I don't want to—but I guess we *do* have to."

Haltingly at first, but gaining facility as I proceeded, I tried to summarize what I'd read. Before long the words were piling into one another with much the same urgency as they had been read.

"The phenomenon of speaking in unknown tongues isn't unique with Christians, Barb. Professor Jennings writes of its occurrence among the Shango Cult in Trinidad, among witch doctors in Africa, among non-Christian American Indians and Eskimos, and among mystics called shamans. The Holy Spirit can't be supplying words to those people."

"The devil imitates the work of God, Bob. Remember Moses before the Pharaoh?"

"Granted. But there are no specifically reported incidents of speaking in unknown tongues in the Old Testament. Yet it *is* reported that the oracles of Delphi spoke in tongues hundreds of years before Pentecost. If this was the work of the devil, he was imitating a miracle that hadn't even occurred yet."

Barbara said nothing, so I continued. "The oracles were highly respected and admired in Greece for a long time. In addition to their supposed prophetic powers, it is said they performed spiritual healings. I don't think it was any accident that it was the church at Corinth, Greece, that so exuberantly practiced speaking in unknown tongues. It was an outward sign the people of that country immediately accepted as proof of spiritual prowess. It was in their history already, quite apart from Christ."

"That doesn't prove that the people of Corinth weren't speaking in tongues as a result of the Holy Spirit."

"No, it doesn't, and I don't know if there *is* a perfectly conclusive way of proving it. But we can't perfectly prove that smoking cigarettes causes cancer in humans, can we? All the signs point to it, however, and we believe it *must* be true!"

Her lips had drawn into a thin line and now she pointed a finger at me menacingly. "Your voice is hard, Bob. I'm warning you. . . ."

"I'm sorry, I'm sorry! I've got all these things on my mind just aching to be said and they're coming out too fast."

"Well, you just cool them off, mister, if you want me to listen!"

With effort I subdued my tone and told her that speaking in unknown tongues had been observed and reported in children as young as three years, in people who had just suffered strokes, and in schizophrenics. "These people were incapable of a conscious surrender of their lives to Jesus Christ with any understanding of what they were doing. Yet there is no evidence the devil used their speaking for evil, either. What are we to gather from that?"

The clock ticked away the minutes as we discussed the three possible origins of glossolalia. Barbara pointed out that there was no way of proving that all speaking in unknown tongues was the same. I agreed, but suggested there could be little comfort drawn from that fact. "For example, your prayer group very likely would accept any person who claimed to be a Christian and who could offer speaking in tongues as a credential, now wouldn't they?"

"If they also showed the fruits of the Spirit in their lives."

"But that could be faked and it would take some time to find out. Now the Antichrist is supposed to gather a following and obtain power by appearing holy and performing miracles. For the sake of argument, let's say one of those miracles is the ability to speak in unknown tongues. Since you can't prove the origin of tongues and since the Antichrist would claim to be from God, he'd very probably receive the support of millions of Pentecostals. That's quite a power base."

"Oh, that's farfetched thinking!"

"Maybe and maybe not. But clearly we shouldn't evaluate people by their ability to speak in unknown tongues. Not when non-Christians, infants, stroke patients, and schizophrenics can do it and we can't tell with certainty where it's coming from."

"You believe the psychological explanation, don't you, Bob?"

"When we are talking about *unknown* tongues, yes. Oh, I fully believe God can repeat Pentecost anytime and anywhere He chooses to do so. I also believe the devil can ape God's works and use it for evil. But in both cases, I believe the speech will be *given* without any effort on the part of the speaker." I lowered my voice and leaned forward. "Barb, more than one of these books said that the onset of tongues is usually stimulated by having the seeker repeat some key word or phrase over and over and over. Was this true in your case?"

She lowered her eyes, looked at her hands, and said very softly, "Yes."

"How did it happen?"

Her voice sounded nervous and uncomfortable. "Well, we were all praying there in the bedroom and some time had passed and still nothing had happened. Holly then told me that some people found it helpful to say a word out loud several times. It was supposed to simply help overcome inhibition."

She paused, so I asked, "What was the word?"

"Hallelujah."

"And it was while repeating this word that your speech changed and became an unknown tongue?"

"Yes."

"Hallelujah, Hallelujah, Hallelujah."

"Bob!"

"You're right, I'm sorry. Barb, Holly is the woman who was in town for just a few weeks, wasn't she?" She nodded, so I continued. "Well, I'd like to tell you about John Kildahl's book. I think you will find some interesting parallels between your experience and his findings."

As gently as I could, I described the human-leader concept Kildahl had discovered and its striking analogy to the hypnotism situation. Then I sketched the personality traits and life situations most often found in tongue speakers.

"You've always had an inferiority complex, Barb; we've talked about it before. There was love, but also a great deal of bickering and arguing in your home as you grew up. It left you with an unsureness about yourself and so you've tended to depend on others. I made life miserable for you over the money situation and you felt like our marriage was falling apart. You prayed about it and nothing changed right away, so you became dissatisfied with your religious life. And here were all these women, many of whom you knew and respected, filled with joy and apparent spiritual power. They had something you didn't and they convinced you that speaking in tongues was the doorway to that 'something.' And then Holly showed up and you were impressed with her especially. If, now, you received the Baptism in the Holy Spirit and started speaking in tongues, perhaps your prayer power would be increased and you could save your marriage. But if that was not granted, at least you would be accepted by this group and have a lot of friends. For a shy person especially, this must have been highly desirable. Knowing now what I do, I think your experience was inevitable."

Tears had welled up in Barbara's eyes as I had talked and in the pause that followed, sobs forced their way to the surface. She trembled with them and then buried her face on the bed with a wailing cry. Her body shook as it all came out in heartrending bursts.

"Darling? Barb?" I moved across the room and sat down beside her on the bed. "I didn't want to make you cry, honest. I just thought you ought to know these things."

The covers muffled her voice but I could still make out what she had said. "Why did He do it?"

"What?"

She half-rolled over and turned tear-streaked cheeks up at me. "Why did He do it? Why? Why?"

I was too bewildered to speak.

"If all that you say is true, Bob, then God let me make a fool of myself. An emotional, silly fool who can be talked into anything! He shouldn't have done that when I was trusting Him!"

"Oh, honey, no!"

"It was all a fake. I just thought I'd had an experience. It didn't mean anything. Nothing at all."

"I think it did."

"You mean you think I proved I could be hypnotized. That's all it really meant, wasn't it?"

"No. No. I think you genuinely were filled by the

Holy Spirit, but that the tongues were something tacked on. I think in some way you were able to transfer the control of your speech from your conscious to your subconscious mind. The conscious mind checks our speech before it lets it out; the subconscious doesn't. Don't blame God for this."

"He could have stopped it! He didn't have to let it happen! Oh. . . ."

"God loves you, Barb. Please don't turn on Him. If I thought this was going to. . . aw, honey, take it out on me somehow, not on Him. Look, I said it couldn't be conclusively proved. All I want you to do is to investigate it. Up until now you've only heard one side of the question. Read books on the other side. Talk to someone besides me about it. See if you get a different picture than I did. If you'll do that and you're still convinced that tongues are from the Holy Spirit, okay. At least your faith in them will be your own and not someone else's."

Thus was the stage set for a not-so-festive Family Day. Anger, resentment, and indignation boiled in Barbara, turning her normally lovely face into a portrait of storm. Any wrong word risked lightning in return—I held my peace. We couldn't cancel the outing because we had promised the kids, but it was obvious they were the only ones who would enjoy it.

Jerry and Judy were more subdued than usual as we drove to the plant. They knew the heavy silence between Barbara and me meant trouble. But they soon forgot about it as we joined the crowds passing through the gates that so seldom opened. Thousands were taking advantage of the rare opportunity, and as I had predicted, the sun was shining brightly.

For the kids it was a circus. Industrial glassblowers held them spellbound as they warmed their wands over Bunsen burners and then puffed out imaginative designs before their eyes. Jerry kept looking for the nonexistent operator of a magnetic tape-controlled milling machine which was cutting and shaping a large block of steel as if by magic. A computer station in one building allowed them to type in questions on a keyboard and then immediately get an answer back on an illuminated display. They both sat in my chair and laughed as they swiveled round and round. In another part of our office, they drew pictures on mylar with felt pens and projected them onto a large screen with a viewgraph machine. Intoxicated as they were with these activities, they didn't notice that their mother said not a word.

The coup-de-grace of the entire day was to observe a rocket sled shot, and for this event temporary grandstands had been erected. The stands were almost full as we came hurrying up. I spotted some seats and ushered the kids quickly toward them before I realized who would be sitting directly behind us. Celia and Frank Beecham! Tongue speakers! But it was too late to change direction.

Their faces brightened when they saw us. "Hi there!" they greeted enthusiastically. I nodded with a half smile, sat down, and wondered what to do next.

Celia said a few words to Barbara, but that apparently dried up quickly, too. The silence was embarrassing. We had been becoming pretty good friends before this tongues business had come up, but the only words that came to my mind now were accusations. I just kept quiet.

It took almost thirty minutes to dispose of formalities and to have the shot, and each one was agonizing. I didn't look around until it was all over, but when I did, Frank and Celia were gone. Scanning the departing crowd proved that they had changed seats. Barbara had probably already told Celia of my reaction to tongues and they had been just as uncomfortable in my presence as I was in theirs.

The kids were happy enough that evening not to grumble when the baby-sitter came. We were to meet Harry and Bess, our oldest and closest friends, for bowling. As it turned out, they were late, so Barbara and I silently drank coffee at a little table and watched the other bowlers perform. With no preliminaries, Barbara suddenly said, "I want to read that book."

"Which one?"

"The one by the psychotherapist. Maybe you're right and *maybe you're not*. I've decided I want to see for myself."

"That's all I ask, Barb. It's at home and I'll get it for you when we get there."

That's all she said about it, but it was enough. I felt confident that she would question tongues herself if exposed to some literature that didn't glamorize them. And after reading Kildahl's book, I was sure she would want to read the others.

Or so I thought.

6

Cease-Fire Number One

Our private war was suspended by unspoken agreement in the days that followed. I had to allow Barbara time to read Kildahl's book and additional time to react to it. Undoubtedly there would be more discussion, but for now the guns must be holstered.

Quickly I hit upon an effective if not commendable scheme to determine when we could reopen our talks. Barbara kept the book on the bedroom dresser and marked her place with a green ribbon. Each night when I came in from work I could check her progress while she was busy in the kitchen. As sneaky as that sounds, it seemed prudent under the circumstances.

I couldn't get Frank and Celia Beecham off my mind. As much as I resented Celia's participation in Barbara's Baptism in the Holy Spirit, it seemed childish and foolish to have snubbed them. A confrontation might have been honorable, at least, but a snub was a cowardly thing.

There was no way of knowing just where all this was leading me. A day might be coming when I would regret that snub for more reasons than just a matter of personal pride. The first thing Monday morning I called Frank, tried to explain the tensions Barbara and I were under that day, and offered an apology. When he accepted it, I felt very much relieved. Thankfully, he chose not to press the matter with me at that time.

The rest of the day I bore down on my work, trying to catch up the stolen hours of the week before. That evening at home my surreptitious check of the green ribbon revealed that Barbara had read three chapters —that seemed a good start. Perhaps it wouldn't take too long for her to finish the book and then we could get some things settled.

About midmorning on Tuesday, Murray Simms unexpectedly dropped in at the office. "Bob, I was going through my books and found this one by the Reverend John R. W. Stott. He is Anglican and I happen to know him personally. I can testify that this man is full of the Holy Spirit if anyone is. I thought you might like to read what he has to say."

It was a small book which was further dwarfed by my rather large hands. I turned it over to see the title —*The Baptism & Fullness of the Holy Spirit.* "Thanks, Murray. I'll get it back to you as soon as I can."

"I think this would be a good book for Barbara to read, if she will. How are things going with you two?"

"Pretty rocky. I'm not the diplomat you are."

"Give God a chance to supply some answers, Bob. Keep praying." He smiled and shook hands. "I've got an appointment—as usual. Keep the book as long as you like."

This time I used the noon hour to read, and with my new-found ability to digest printed pages quickly, I finished it during that period. Murray was right; the book was the most sensitive yet penetrating dissent that I'd read. Like Hoekema, Stott recommended tolerance toward those who practiced tongues. Later I would wish that these recommendations had truly penetrated into my prejudiced mind. I placed the book in my lunch box to remember to take it home. Barbara would like this one.

That evening I attended an organizational meeting of a parents' group concerned with Jerry's and Judy's elementary school. The school administration was trying out some new concepts which were not proving to be effective, and we felt a unified voice was necessary to suggest some constructive changes. Since our efforts were not without opposition, this activity promised to require a considerable amount of time from Barbara and me in the days ahead. Before going to the meeting, however, I'd noted the green ribbon had moved ahead one more chapter and I was pleased.

The next day I was leafing through some briefing aids when the thought struck me that I wasn't being very thorough. At this point I had read five books and one article that dissented from the Pentecostal doctrine, but only John Sherrill's book that advocated it. Shouldn't I study the books that were passed hand to hand among Barbara's prayer-group members? Wouldn't these authors' words be quoted to me when finally, and it seemed inevitably, I would be trapped into a discussion of tongues with someone other than Barbara? Yes, I needed to broaden my study.

I ate my lunch while driving to our church. Surely our little library would have some of the titles. But no, there were no titles whatsoever on the subject, either pro or con. That seemed strange now that I knew of so many tongue speakers in our congregation. Then the first of many fantasies set in on me. Of course! To donate books concerning tongue speaking to the church library would bring the subject out in the open and possibly stimulate the donation of dissenting books. On the other hand, to remain semisecret and circulate advocating books hand to hand to selected individuals would allow new believers to be recruited without worrisome opposition. Once there were enough believers, well. . . .

Dark thoughts of a Pentecostal take-over of our congregation haunted me as I pulled the pickup into the parking lot of the Christian Supply Center. The enigmatic saleslady brightened up considerably as I laid Dennis Bennett's *Nine O'Clock in the Morning* and Larry Christenson's *Speaking in Tongues* on the counter.

"These are good books; I've read them myself. You're quite interested in this subject, aren't you?"

I smiled at the irony of it. "Yes."

"Oh, Mr. Samuelson's here if you'd like to see him."

Arnie Samuelson turned out to be a large man who gave the impression of always being in a hurry. When I explained what I wanted, he was able to guide me to a couple of titles I hadn't discovered on my own and said he would order a third that wasn't on his shelves. All in all, however, he was no more enthusiastic than his saleslady had been. A second fantasy asserted itself: this bookstore was primarily Pentecostal and my ordered book would probably never arrive.

Barbara was involved now with circulating a petition for the parents' group at the school, so I wasn't too surprised when I found the green ribbon hadn't moved that evening or the next. I occupied my time by reading the Pentecostal books. Feeling as I did, it was difficult to read dispassionately—as a matter of fact, it was impossible. To relieve the anger that rose and fell within me, I made bitter marginal notes at great length. All the old fears intensified and kindling was piled on my flaming new fantasies by these emotional testimonials.

Never had I seen the phenomenon of speaking in unknown tongues lauded, glamorized, and promoted with such vigor! In spite of the fact that Saint Paul listed the gift of tongues and their interpretation in last place in 1 Corinthians 12:4-10, the authors spotlighted these gifts as if they were indeed the keys to eternity. To have read these books noncritically would have left the reader totally convinced that tongues must be a "shazam!" that turns ordinary people into superchristians! Barbara had told me that her group considered tongues as one of the least of the spiritual gifts (a contestable assertion in itself under the circumstances); these authors obviously weren't members of *her* group. Or did her group just say that?

The more I read, the more I was convinced that my

opposition to the Charismatic Movement must be on a larger scale than simply talking with Barbara. The Pentecostals were well organized, had their own press, and were enjoying phenomenal success among mainline denominational congregations by using the small extrachurch group technique. Our own congregation had been successfully infiltrated already without the knowledge, apparently, of most of its members. If our clergy were aware of it, I realized they would have to take a position of tolerance. Therefore, if our church were to be prevented from gradually adopting Pentecostalism, a layman would have to lead the opposition. That layman might as well be me.

A vague plan of attack—or counterattack as I thought of it—started forming in my mind. First and foremost I must change my own wife's mind about speaking in tongues and make her my ally. Second, I must take issue with the new Pentecostals (or Neo-Pentecostals as they are sometimes called) whenever I overheard them espousing their doctrine in our church. And third, I must somehow make the rest of our congregation aware of what was going on. That meant I needed some kind of a forum. There were many possibilities, but one of absolute necessity was to place dissenting books in our library. First, though, Barbara.

The same place was marked in Kildahl's book when I arrived home Friday evening and that was a bit irritating. Surely there had been *some* time during the day for Barbara to have read a bit. The church newspaper had arrived in the mail so I sat down with it to await dinner. In a moment I stiffened and sat forward to read a particular announcement on the front page.

CELEBRATION OF PENTECOST! the headline shouted, to be held the following evening, May 20, in our church's Fellowship Hall. It was signed by the chairman of our Commission on Evangelism, a man I knew now to be a tongue speaker! To my knowledge, this would be the first intrusion as a group the tongue speakers had made on our church property. Nowhere in the article was speaking in tongues mentioned by name—that was carefully omitted—but everywhere it was implied. A scriptural reference was given to Romans 8:26, joy and the Holy Spirit were emphasized, and at the end was the Pentecostal salute "Praise the Lord!" It couldn't have been more obvious to anyone who had been exposed to the Charismatic Movement.

Now I was in a bind. Barbara, I thought, would want to go and be with her friends. I had *no* intention of going myself, but did I have a right to forbid her? No, of course not. If I ever hoped to influence her opinions on this subject any further, there was only one thing I could do.

I showed her the article at the dinner table. "Barb, if you want to go, please do so. I'll keep the kids and won't make a fuss."

She didn't answer immediately, but instead studied the announcement. "No, I don't think I will. You don't *really* want me to go and I'm not sure what I believe myself right now."

Naturally I didn't protest!

A pile of chores had accumulated for both of us and

we spent most of the weekend performing them. We did return to the Sunday-school class for the first time in three weeks. I was tense and almost got into an argument with the discussion leader, but real trouble was averted. I kept staring at all the faces as if they were strangers. It was still incredible to me that so many of these people had accepted the Pentecostal doctrine; I wondered how many of them *knew* there was another side to the story the Pentecostals told. When Barbara finished that book. . . .

Monday and Tuesday passed and still the little green ribbon didn't advance. Pressure was building up inside me and I wondered how long I could hold my silence. Then on Wednesday, Barbara hit me with a bombshell!

"Bob, I've decided to give up speaking in tongues for the good of our family. I had a long talk with Betty today—you know, our neighbor up the street. She says that speaking in tongues is definitely one of the least of the spiritual gifts and if it is causing division and strife in our family, then I should give it up. She says that God never intends to have one of his gifts cause trouble between people and I have to agree with that. I truly never meant to bring home so much trouble."

I was speechless.

"Aren't you happy about it?"

"Well . . . yes, I guess I am. Barb, are you giving it up because you've changed your mind about tongues, or simply to placate me?"

"I'm not sure what I believe about them now. But I'm sick of this tension, this fighting. I don't want our home to be a battleground."

She *hadn't* changed her mind, not really. This didn't fit in with my plans at all. You can't be neutral about speaking in tongues—you either believe in them or you don't. I needed Barbara as an ally.

"Barb, I appreciate what you're trying to do for us, but I still wish you would read Kildahl's book. I think before this is all over, you're going to have to be very sure of what you believe—one way or the other. Won't you do that? Please?"

An expression of pain came on her face. "All right, if you want me to so badly. But there isn't much time these days what with the parents' group and all. . . ."

Another countdown began. I tried my best to be patient, but time was passing and the Pentecostals seemed to be gaining a stronger and stronger foothold at our church. Little wonder, since there was no opposition.

The weekend came and went and still Barbara made no further progress on the book. There was always a good excuse, one after another after another. On Monday, I bought another advocating book: *Catholic Pentecostals* by Kevin and Dorothy Ranaghan. The evangelizing message was so passionately worded in this book I became alarmed. There seemed to be no claims at all which the tongue speakers would not make for the phenomenon! The pressure to retaliate kept building and building. And still the green ribbon did not move.

A new and nasty fantasy started growing in my mind. Though I tried not to believe it, it tenaciously hung on and taunted me. Grief was to be *its* blossom.

Then Thursday came. It was the first day of June and Barbara felt a little ill. She decided to spend the day resting in bed and I knew this was it! With no appointments, no distractions, she would surely have time to finish the book, if by no other means than between naps. I was one of the first out of the factory parking lot that evening, so eager was I to get home and talk about it.

Barbara was in her robe but working in the kitchen when I arrived. She said nothing about the book when we greeted one another, so as soon as I could, I went to the bedroom and checked it.

The little green ribbon was still nestled at the end of chapter four! I stared at it in disbelief, then flipped forward through the pages to see if she had made any marginal notes. None! She hadn't read the book—she hadn't even touched it. All day long with very little else to do she hadn't read a single page!

Whatever barrier there is that holds back our tempers snapped in me at that moment. I could feel my face getting hot. I clenched and unclenched my fists. Then I moved back toward the kitchen with trouble at the controls.

7

Scream Murder!

"Barb!"

I started hollering before I'd even rounded the hall-way corner. "Barb!"

"My goodness, what is it?" She was sitting in the den waiting while a casserole baked.

I sat down heavily beside her on the divan. The single cushion bounced her up a bit as my weight hit the other end. "Barb, didn't you read any of Kildahl's book today?"

"Oh . . . no, I didn't."

"Well, why didn't you?"

"Are you mad?"

"Yes, I'm mad! You said you wanted to read that book and I've been waiting almost three weeks to discuss it with you."

"Bob, the whole subject has become very painful to me. I didn't feel well today so I tried to read some things to cheer me up. A book on tongue speaking wasn't what I needed."

"Well, what about all the other days?"

"You know how busy I've been!"

"Oh, sure. You were busy back in March and April too. But you weren't too busy to read all those Pentecostal books, were you? That was different, wasn't it? Those women you wanted so much to be friends with gave you *those* books, didn't they? It didn't take you very long to read *them!*"

The irish was in her eyes again. "I don't like your tone, Bob. I don't like it at all!"

"Well, I don't care whether you like it or not, Barb! I've been holding my temper for three weeks while you've been letting that book go to rot. What are you planning to do anyway, bury your head in the sand and pretend the Charismatic Movement doesn't exist anymore? It won't *work*, Barb; we're surrounded by it. Our Sunday-school class, our church, our neighborhood is plagued with it! I've been keeping quiet, trying to give you a chance to study and make up your mind about it, but I'm not going to keep quiet much longer!"

"What do you mean by that?"

"I mean I'm going to fight it however and whenever I can! I think it's counterfeit, I think it's a spiritual con game, and I think our congregation has a right to know what's going on!"

"You still think it's evil in some way, don't you? Your pride is hurt because your wife went out and did something you didn't approve of and didn't even bother to ask you! Why, you're acting as if . . . as if I were unfaithful to you! And now you want me to join you in some sort of personal vendetta against all those who were involved. Well, I won't do it!"

I shook my head in confirmation. "That's what I thought!"

"What do you mean?"

"All that big talk about giving up tongues for the sake of the family. *You haven't quit, have you?* You just do it when I'm at work, or when you go to visit one of your Pentecostal friends. What was it you said, you can even pray in tongues to yourself? I'll bet you've been doing it when I was not more than three feet away. Oh, that's great! This way you can pacify your husband and still have all your new friends patting you on the back, too!"

Tears spilled out on her cheeks. "That's not true!"

"Why not? All this *started* in deception. Why not add a little white lie to it and come out the winner both ways?"

"No, no, no! I didn't lie to you! I've never lied to you! Why are you doing this to me?"

White hot anger had full control of me now. "Why are *you* doing this to *me?* Why didn't you talk to me before you consented to this so-called Baptism in the Holy Spirit? Why didn't you read Kildahl's book? Why don't you want me to speak out against tongues? I'll tell you why not. Because you're more loyal to those babbling buddies of yours than you are to *me!* Because to spread this doctrine they have to keep it *under-ground!* Because *you'll* look bad if it's *your* husband who. . . ."

"Eeeeeeeeee . . . eeeeeeah!"

Her scream stopped me in midsentence. She had

jumped to her feet, tears streaming out of red-streaked eyes.

"Eeeeeeeeee . . . eeeeeeah!"

The piercing sound filled the room, bounced off the walls, cut right through me. "Oh no!" I thought. "Oh no, no, no!"

"You don't believe me! You'll never believe me now! Eeeeeeeeeeeee . . . eeeeeeeah!"

I scrambled to my feet and started toward her.

"No! Don't you touch me! Eeeeeeeeee . . . eeeeeeah! You'll just tell me that everything's going to be all right and it will *never* be all right again! Eeeeeeeeeeeeeeeee . . . eeeeeeeeeeah! Eeeeeeeeeeeee . . . eeeeeeeeeeah!"

The terrifying sound attenuated slightly as she ran to our bedroom and slammed the door shut behind her. Bewildered, trembling, I slumped back onto the divan. Oh dear God Almighty, what have I done? My lower lip started quivering and, quite out of control of myself, tears started down my own cheeks. Soon I was crying like a baby.

The casserole burned.

I don't know how long I remained there in the den. Sometime later I heard Barbara slam out of the house, a car motor started, and tires squealed on pavement. I didn't even look up.

I didn't want our marriage to end, but it seemed too much to hope that I hadn't just murdered it. As darkness fell, I wondered where the kids were.

8

Stripped of My White Charger

The telephone felt cold and lifeless in my hand as a voice at the other end said, "Reverend Fellows? Yes, just a moment please."

I was too worn out to even drum my fingernails as I waited for our pastor to come to the phone. It was Friday morning and I was finally taking a suggestion Barbara had made some time earlier. Perhaps it was too late now, but I had nothing else left.

"Hello?" The bass voice of Ken Fellows boomed through my earpiece.

"Reverend Fellows, this is Bob Branch."

"Oh, yes, Bob. How are you?"

"Not so well, sir, and that's why I'm calling. Do you know . . . that is, are you familiar with the Charismatic Movement, or Renewal, or Revival, whatever you wish to call it?"

"Oh, yes."

I don't know why I should have been surprised, but I was. "Well, I have a personal problem connected with it and I was wondering if . . . that is, could you. . . ."

"Do you want to tell me about it privately?"

I sighed with relief. "Yes, sir, that's it exactly."

"How about today over lunch? I could meet you at that restaurant near the factory."

"That would be just fine, sir. Perfect in fact. Twelve noon?"

"Fine! I'll see you then."

I replaced the telephone on its cradle and stared into space. Barbara had gotten home safely and the kids had come in on their own. It was no thanks to me. In fact, none of this whole rotten business would have happened except for me. Those screams had surely pounded that home. I heard them all night long. I could still hear them echoing, echoing in my head.

In no time at all, it seemed, I was looking over a checkered tablecloth at the smiling face of Reverend Fellows. He was a big man and twenty years my senior, but he'd lost none of his vitality or zest for life. He seemed intensely interested in everything and everyone, and immediately I felt comfortable with him.

"Maybe I'd better ask you first of all, Reverend Fellows, do you believe in speaking in unknown tongues?"

"Oh, call me Ken," he chided with a smile. "I don't particularly believe 'against' them, Bob, but I don't speak in tongues personally, if that's what you mean."

That was a relief at least. "Are you aware that many members of our congregation *do* speak in tongues?"

"Yes, of course. I think I know just who they are, too. But it's only a small fraction of our total membership, Bob. Is that what you're worried about?"

I stared at him with new respect. "Partly, yes. You

see, I've been reading some books by Pentecostal authors and it seems to me that they get carried away both by the importance of tongues and the need to spread their practice. I'm aware now of these groups operating in our own church and it *does* worry me. They seem like . . . like some sort of secret society! Many people don't even know they're there. *I* didn't know they existed until a few weeks ago. Ken, I don't believe in tongues and I feel like I should do something about it." I then told him of my boyhood exposure to tongue speakers.

When I'd finished, Ken thoughtfully twirled his fork and then pointed it at me. "This fork, Bob, is a marvelous utensil to help us eat, but if I plunge it into your chest, it becomes an instrument of murder. That isn't the fault of the fork, but of its user. Tongues can be abused, too, and I've seen it in my own experience. That isn't to say that the practice of tongues cannot be beneficial, however. Now you take the tongue speakers in our church, for example. They are some of the happiest, most dedicated, hardest-working members we have. There is no question in my mind that they have a vital relationship with Christ and God. As their pastor, could I hope for more? Our church, and now I'm speaking of the larger church, has traditionally steered away from dogma, has encouraged a climate in which different opinions can exist without fear of censure—provided, of course, that these opinions don't contradict the life and teachings of our Lord Jesus. It is one of my duties to ensure that this tradition is continued in our local church. Therefore, I will not condemn speaking in tongues in our congregation as long as it bears fruit for our Lord. Neither will I allow a group to impose this doctrine on those in the church who don't want it."

"Has anyone approached you along these lines?"

"Yes, I had one group come in and express displeasure with the format of our worship services. Some of their criticisms were good ones; some were not, in my opinion. We've changed some, but we'll not change completely, at least not while I'm pastor."

"I've thought, Ken, that I should seek some forum within our church to oppose the Charismatic influence, but I don't want to be the cause of a schism. In your capacity as our spiritual leader, could you tell me if there *is* such a forum?"

He thought briefly before saying, "No."

"None at all?"

"None at all, Bob. I wouldn't want you to do that."

I breathed deeply, half in disappointment and half in a strange sort of relief. Then I leaned forward. "But don't you think it's wrong for our members to get only half a story—the Pentecostal half? These groups provide potential converts with all kinds of books which advocate tongue speaking. Who gives them a book that disagrees with it? I've thought that I'd like to donate some dissenting books to our library so that our members could get the other half of the story. Would there be anything wrong with that?"

He munched pensively on a carrot while I waited expectantly. "How about donating some of *each* kind, both pro and con, in equal numbers? I think that's the only fair way I could accept them."

"That's a deal." I didn't have much to lose with such an arrangement. The pro books had already been widely read by hand to hand circulation anyway. Most people didn't even know the con books existed.

I toyed with my food for awhile, my head down. Ken must have been studying me for the next thing I heard from him was, "Well?"

"Well what?"

"Well you said that what we just discussed was only a part of your problem. What comes next?"

"Oh, yes." I fumbled for some clever words, found none, so simply blurted out, "Barbara, my wife, started speaking in tongues about a month ago."

"Oh! I didn't know that." His mind raced. "And you've had some trouble over it? Maybe a great deal of trouble?"

"Yes."

"Well, if you'd like to, why not tell me the whole story?"

So I did. It took some time, of course, but I'd already arranged for an extra-long lunch hour with my boss. I'd stay late to make it up.

When I finished, Ken asked me, "How long have you and Barbara been married, Bob?"

"About twelve and a half years."

"And do you still love her?"

"I guess you couldn't discern it from what I've just

told you, but the answer is yes, very much so. Only I really blew it last night."

"If you'll permit me to say so, you've taken your eye off what is important and permanent and most precious in your life and fixed it on something trivial by comparison. Whatever satisfaction you might gain by winning an argument over speaking in tongues can never replace the lifetime of love you might lose in the process. *Think,* Bob! Think of what all the rest of your life would be like without Barbara!"

"I *do* think of it," I said miserably, "Especially since last night. I hurt her so *badly,* Ken. If you could have heard those screams. . . . But I also think about that young man running down the street in the middle of the night. I think about the sounds I heard through my bedroom window night after horrible night, and of that boy lying on the street corner twitching. I think about the stories I heard about people foaming at the mouth and rolling back and forth on the floor. How do I get rid of those thoughts?"

He looked at me very intently. "I *know* how, Bob, but you won't like it very much."

"How then?"

"You must go to a Pentecostal meeting. You have all the symptoms of unvarnished fear, and you must confront the source of that fear to ever get rid of it. Tongue speakers are what you fear, so you must go to one of their meetings and sit all the way through it, even if you have to go outside and throw up afterwards. Once you've proven to yourself you can survive that experience, you won't fear it anymore. Then these pictures from the past will fade away."

He must have been right because I suddenly felt extremely uncomfortable. "Well—oh, boy—I don't know whether I could do that or not. No, sir, I just don't know."

"Well, whatever else you do, make it up with Barbara. It may take a while, so be patient. I'll be glad to talk to her if she'd like. You'll need all the help the Lord can give you, Bob, so don't forget to ask for it. It sounds to me as if you've been neglecting that lately, and you can see where it's led you. Remember that He promises help to all who ask believing they'll receive. Put Him to the test and see how He can deliver! If speaking in tongues is helping Barbara, don't oppose it, Bob, but instead leave it in the Lord's hands and trust Him to take the fear out of *you*."

"You know, I've received that same advice before. Maybe it's time I took it."

He smiled broadly and I could feel his confidence that everything would straighten out. I wanted so much to feel the same way!

After he'd left, I sat in the pickup a long time adding up the score of my investigation. It was time to be honest, to be brutally honest. My marriage was on the line, perhaps even my sanity—and Barbara's.

None of the material I'd read and none of the people I'd talked to supported in any way my fear that a tongue speaker gradually lost all control of the phenomenon. It must not be true. The *abuse* of tongue speaking, then, must be an individual matter which has to be individually considered.

I hadn't believed Barbara when she told me she'd quit the prayer group and even had given up the practice of tongues. If these things weren't true, however, would she have screamed? And if she had indeed given up both the group and the experience, it meant she hadn't been a puppet of either as I'd imagined.

The hardest thing of all to admit to myself was that the tongue speaking *hadn't really hurt Barbara.* Whatever else I believed about the Baptism in the Holy Spirit and the tongues phenomenon, it had actually *improved* her personality in many respects! *I* was the one who hurt her!

I mentally kicked myself for ever becoming an engineer. Why did I have to choose a discipline that forced me to acknowledge the truth when I saw it?

And now Ken came along and recommended tolerance, as had Hoekema, and Stott, and Murray Simms before him. Ken was well aware of the Pentecostal penetration into our congregation and was dealing with it already, far more sensibly than I could. Gently but firmly he had stripped me of helmet, lance, and white charger. Then to this knight in underwear, he had given but one real charge—to *love* his wife!

I remembered when I was a boy and the dread I'd felt when I knew I had to visit the doctor. Yet after the visit came that wonderful exhilarating release from tension. I started to feel it now.

For the first time in weeks, I also felt like praying. I

lowered my head there in the parking lot and said, "Lord, I've been a trial to You, to my wife, and to many others lately. Please teach me to forgive. And have mercy upon me, a poor sinner."

9

Cease-Fire Number Two

Our dates had always been unorthodox. We'd spent the day one time in episodes of trivia that seemed fantastically exciting. One moment we watched a bait-casting contest at a city lake with anglers attempting to plunk lead weights into brightly colored hoops floating on the water's surface. The next moment we discovered the very *first* 7-11 Store, as it said on a bronze plaque out front, and shared a pint of chocolate ice cream together to celebrate that event. Later we were at a park soaring higher and higher as we pumped and coaxed our swings to greater achievement. Youth, life, love—we had it all together then.

I thought of the happiness that had been on Barbara's face that day as she laughed and swung, her long brown hair fanning out in the breeze behind her. It now seemed so long since she had smiled—but what had I given her to smile about?

I pointed the pickup homeward and hoped someone would be there. An empty house, a penned note taped to the door, sterile quietness—that was what I deserved, I knew. But God is the giver of good gifts and none of us deserve them. Maybe. . . .

Why had it all been so important to me? Had I really been all that concerned with Barbara's welfare? How *could* I have been and hurt her the way I did? Wasn't it really the fear that drove me? Nothing could be more important to me than Barbara!

Unconsciously, I bore down on the accelerator. I was already straining my eyes for a sight of our house before I'd rounded the last corner. Would it . . . yes! The car was there! Maybe. . . .

As soon as I was in the doorway, I called out, "Barb?"

My heart sank when no answer came. But I was simply too impatient.

"Yes?"

There she was in the kitchen, working on our dinner as if it were any other evening. "Oh Barb! Thank You, Lord!"

"What is it, Bob? What's the matter?" Alarm had flashed onto her face.

I tried to answer but broke into an involuntary nervous laugh instead. "Nothing, it's nothing." When the reaction wore off, I said, "It's just that I didn't know if you'd be here. I was afraid you'd be gone."

She looked down at the bowl in which she was mixing biscuit dough. "I wouldn't go without telling you, Bob."

I stood and looked at her drawn face, her unsmiling lips, and my heart bled. When we had first met, Barbara had just started her first teaching assignment.

She had bubbled with life and enthusiasm. Her gaiety had been irrepressible; she had laughed at my cynicism until I had had to laugh, too, and lost it. Was this spirit just submerged, or had I killed it?

Suddenly I was with her at an altar. My knees trembled within my navy blue wool suit, but Barb stood tall and poised beside me, radiantly beautiful in the sequined white gown her mother and aunts had made with love in every stitch. Her hand rested on mine as the pastor had me say, "I, Robert, take thee, Barbara, to be my wedded wife, to have and to hold, from this day forward, for better for worse, for richer for poorer, in sickness and in health, to love and to cherish, till death us do part, and thereto I plight thee my faith."

To love and to cherish! Tears blurred my eyes momentarily. I sat down at the bar across from where she was working. My voice was low as I said, "Barb, I've been a blundering idiot for a month now. Today, though, I finally did something right. It was a suggestion you made to me a long time ago; I had a long talk with Reverend Fellows."

Her hand hesitated in the mixing bowl, but she didn't say anything.

"He told me to knock it off, to quit giving you and everyone else a hard time. But most of all, he made me see just how important you are to me."

She was still silent.

"I don't know how to adequately apologize to you, Barb. I don't know how to make you believe that I'm really, really sorry for all I've said and done to hurt you, except to change. I wouldn't blame you if you chose not to stick around and *see* that change, but I hope you will. I pray you will."

The girl in the swing; the girl at the altar. Could it be again? Dear God, I beg of Thee!

"I love you, Barb."

It wasn't going to happen. I had shoved too hard, pushed too far. That beautiful thing, that precious thing was gone. Murdered!

I sighed and started to rise and leave, but as I did, a floured hand went down on mine, a hand with a silver band about one finger, a hand urgent in its warmth. "Bob?"

A tremble was in her voice. I lifted my eyes to hers, hoping, yet not daring to hope anymore. Mists stood between us.

"Bob, I love you, too! *Oh, I really do!*"

She squeezed hard on my hand and I moved around the bar, took her in my arms, and held on for dear life. "Barb! Darling, I'm so sorry!" We clung to one another —passing heartbeats and crying without shame.

To love and to cherish! To love and to cherish! It rang through my brain, driving out all else.

When I was a young man in college, I angrily left a date one evening and throttled my automobile down the road toward home. The car went faster and faster the more I fumed over the argument. Suddenly, as if out of nowhere, barricades blocked the road ahead, large signs shouted DETOUR, and banks of arrows pointed urgently to the left. The two lanes were quickly narrowing into one which then broke sharply into an S turn.

I jerked my thoughts away from my hurt feelings and hit the brakes hard, but in an orgy of screaming tires and burning rubber, the car skidded into the detour entirely too fast. The center of gravity shifted, the car went up on its outside wheels, and for what seemed an eternity I literally hung between life and death. Finally, the car plopped down safely on all fours again, leaped forward momentarily when the skid broke, and then slowly eased to a stop on the shoulder. I had cut off the ignition and sat there in the darkness for a full hour, allowing tires and brakes and engine and nerves to cool.

Blinded by anger over a trivial quarrel, I had almost sacrificed all the rest of my life in that incident. I'd taken my eyes off the essential thing and indulged my momentarily hurt feelings with dangerous recklessness.

Now, many years later, I had done it again. With the same senseless rashness, I had badgered my wife about speaking in tongues until she'd screamed out in frustration and our marriage had wavered on the brink of dissolution. But God had granted the mercy I'd begged Him for.

Tongues were secondary with us now, as they should have been from the beginning. Wounds required attention. The weekend was a blur of love and tenderness and apology and reconciliation. Barbara and I both recognized how close had been our escape from marital disaster and we clung to one another as to a life ring. Jerry and Judy joined in, too, so happy were they to see some peace and affection in our home again. This was to be no simple truce—this was war's end.

A business trip took me out of state all the following week and I was miserable at the separation. Shortly after I returned, my niece came to visit as part of a prearranged graduation present. As we entertained her, we celebrated our own reunion.

Barbara drove my niece to her home and then continued on with Jerry and Judy to visit her parents. I was to have the house to myself for the next couple of weeks. On parting early that morning, I held each of them longer than usual. "I'm really going to miss you guys. Hurry home!"

Barbara's eyes sparkled with love in the dim predawn light. "We will, darling. We will!"

10

Breakthrough!

If any doubt remained in my mind that God was truly operating in our lives now, it was quickly dispelled. The very day Barbara and the kids left on their trip, I received a call at the office from the Christian Supply Center.

"The book you ordered has arrived, Mr. Branch. You can pick it up anytime."

Another fantasy exploded!

But it was the next morning when I was reading the newspaper that the greater surprise came. A black-bordered advertisement proclaimed that the Full Gospel Business Men's Fellowship was to hold a regional convention at one of the nicer hotels in our city the following weekend. Kenneth Hagin, Sherwin McCurdy, Hilton Sutton, and George Otis were to be the speakers. EVERYONE WELCOME!

Those last words leaped out at me like a command. By now I recognized from my reading that the Full Gospel Business Men's Fellowship was one of the prime movers of the Pentecostal doctrine. Much of the success of the Charismatic Movement has been attributed to the efforts of this organization. If I were to go face-to-face with my fear of tongue speakers, I could hardly pick a better arena in which to confront it.

But I didn't *want* to. My skin prickled just to think of it. Two such meetings had been described in the books I'd read and that was as close as I wanted to get to it. I covered up the advertisement by turning the page.

Then the Reverend Kenneth Fellows got into the act somehow. His words pounded through to me again, "You *must* go to a Pentecostal meeting, Bob!" In my mind I could see him pointing to the advertisement and nodding his head yes.

"C'mon, Ken," I thought in rebellion, "this is the big leagues! How about that Charismatic group over at the Catholic church, or the one that meets at the university? Wouldn't they do just as well?"

The imaginary head shook an emphatic no!

"It's got to be this one, huh? I was afraid you'd feel that way!" I reluctantly reexamined the advertisement.

Meetings were scheduled for Thursday, Friday, and Saturday nights. I chose Thursday, June 29, thinking that they might not be fully warmed up on the first evening. I needed whatever edge I could get!

It would be easier with Barbara out of town. If we had gone to such a meeting together, she might take any sign of displeasure on my part as a tacit slap at herself. She had been slapped too much already.

The week went by much too quickly. Butterflies fluttered in my stomach every time I thought about it, reminiscent of high-school football days.

I arrived at the hotel fifteen minutes early that Thursday evening and spent the waiting time praying in my pickup. "Lord, You know how scared I am. Make my feet move me to that meeting and tell my stomach to behave. Please turn out the coward that is within me. Thank You, Lord."

I pushed my feet out onto the pavement. My legs felt rubbery as I walked. At the front door I hesitated momentarily, then plunged inside. I felt like I had just been prodded off the end of the plank.

Table after table of literature and tapes for sale lined the corridor leading to the auditorium. I passed a group of about ten men in business suits who were in a football-style huddle. Their arms were linked and they were all praying out loud, in tongues, I supposed, since I didn't understand any of the words. Just after I passed, they broke up with a chorus of Praise-the-Lords.

I found a seat about halfway back and tried to look inconspicuous. A quartet was playing gospel songs. Here and there people were greeting one another with hugs, kisses, and slaps on the back. I pulled out a notebook and pen. Perhaps it would help me get through the proceedings if I recorded what happened.

The quartet sang for about thirty minutes and then invited the crowd to sing along with them for another thrity minutes. Most of the crowd clapped their hands in time with the music and swayed slightly from side to side. At the end of every song would come one or more Praise-the-Lords from the audience and the song leaders alike.

Kenneth Hagin was to be the featured speaker of the evening, I learned, and he was noted for spiritual healings. In keeping with this theme, I supposed, a man from the audience went forward and testified how his eye condition, brought on by sugar diabetes, had been miraculously healed overnight by God. His testimony was interrupted several times by more Praise-the-Lords. Some people raised both their hands over their heads when they said this. I was later to learn that this is a common Pentecostal prayer position.

Next came a long series of short speeches by the many people seated at the head table, most of them presidents of Full Gospel Business Men's Fellowship locals. There was general praying in unknown tongues during nearly every speech, but no interpretation was offered. I wondered what had happened to Saint Paul's instructions about tongue speaking in 1 Corinthians 14, especially with regards to two or three at the most speaking, one at a time, always with interpretation. This was often a general roar of tongues.

The note-taking technique was working. I was so engrossed in observing and analyzing the proceedings, I didn't think about my fears.

The man who must have been called the master of ceremonies made the final preliminary speech. This was a real table-beater. He said people belonging to many denominations didn't have any spiritual power because it wasn't taught to them. "So bring 'em here!" he shouted, and the crowd roared its approval. He then exhorted those present to buy the books and to buy the tapes, take them back to the prayer groups in their own churches, and "spread the word!"

Two hours and ten minutes had passed before Kenneth Hagin was introduced. I looked around the auditorium. It was packed with hundreds and hundreds of people. I stretched to relieve my cramped muscles.

Hagin talked for another hour and five minutes. He opened with about ten minutes of a machine-gun style, sing-song monologue that you had to be extremely quick to follow. He testified that Jesus appeared to him, led him before the throne of God, and that both God and Jesus talked to him and commanded him to heal. He made a lot of jokes and particularly seemed to enjoy ridiculing those who didn't believe in tongues, much to the delight of the crowd. Finally, he called for all those who wanted to be healed to come forward.

Three hours and fifteen minutes had passed by now and my joints were screaming. I leaned forward and asked the man in front of me how long this would continue. He smiled and said, "Why, this may go on all night!" That did it; Friday was a workday. When the audience stood for a song, I slipped out the back and headed for the door.

Outside the night was cool and clear. I groaned and stretched and did a couple of knee bends. Then it hit me. I had done it! I had really done it! I had faced the

Pentecostals! "Thank You, Lord! Thank You!" Millions of stars twinkled merrily down on me as I skipped to my pickup.

Everyone at work the next day was baffled by my general exuberance, but I offered no explanations. My doctor visit was behind me and I felt great! Ho, boy!

About midafternoon, I got another wild idea. Friday night was the evening for the Charismatic group meeting at the Catholic church. Many of our neighbors and church members had attended that one. If I could face the Full Gospel Business Men's Fellowship convention, surely I could face *this* prayer meeting. Why not?

I called our neighbor Betty, who was a Catholic, to get the starting time. I think she was a bit astounded that I should be asking.

That evening I was one of the first at the church. The meeting was to be held in the gymnasium and two- or three-hundred folding chairs were arranged for circular seating. The prayer-group leader, along with several guitarists, sat in the innermost circle.

The format was considerably different, in keeping with the prayer-group nature of the meeting. The first fifteen minutes were devoted to singing and the same handclapping and swaying motion occurred. Immediately thereafter, however, the leader called for everyone to relax, to focus their thoughts on Jesus, and to allow the Spirit to move among them.

There was a momentary silence and then a group started singing softly in tongues to no particular melody. It was done sensitively and did have an element of beauty to it, as Barbara had said. This died away, there was another pause, and then a slow song in English was sung by the guitar group.

This singing in tongues and singing in English alternated for awhile, and then someone in the back of the room said four or five sentences very loudly in a tongue. There were three interpretations in English given by others in the group; all the interpretations differed from one another and all were known Bible verses.

The rest of the meeting was characterized by singing and prayers in both tongues and in English. The tone was much gentler than the one at the convention. On two occasions, individuals asked the group to pray for specific personal needs, which both times brought forth a flurry of tongue praying. At another point, a woman fainted and had to be taken out. The group was assured that it was nothing serious.

After the meeting, which had lasted about an hour and a half, I made my way to the group leader, introduced myself, and asked why the group violated Paul's regulations (at least *six* loud outbursts of tongues had occurred, and none of the general tongue praying or singing was interpreted). He replied that they had found the regulations impractical when so large a group was present.

Those who wanted instruction in Baptism in the Holy Spirit were led to smaller rooms off the main hall. As I left, I noticed a tableful of Pentecostal books that were being offered for sale, the same books I had seen at the hotel.

That evening at home I stayed up late, reflecting on

all that I'd seen in these two meetings and attempting to put them in perspective. There were things said that I agreed with, and many others that I didn't agree with at all. But one thing was absolutely clear—Reverend Fellows had been 100 percent correct about me. My fear was gone, the feelings of danger had evaporated, and at long last I could look at the Charismatic Movement objectively. Only through grace had I kept Barbara while I was groping to find myself.

I cocked my head to one side and listened for a few minutes. Yes, oh yes, even the past was quiet!

11

State of the Union

Some months have passed now since that jolting day in May when I first learned my wife was speaking in tongues. We have hit a few more bumps on our return to domestic normalcy, but none so unsettling as those I've already described. Today, there is a new maturity evident in our home.

Barbara and I both have gained a keener awareness of the flowerlike fragility of a good marriage. Our experiences drove home the truth that everything one marriage partner does or thinks has an effect on the other. Two becoming one is no idle phrase! Because we came so close to separation, we are much more sensitive now to each other's needs, desires, and beliefs.

Every marriage suffers a bit as the demands and distractions of everyday life slowly and almost imperceptibly add tarnish to the original romance. Our experience scoured away these stains of complacency and allowed us to see one another in the same precious light of first affection. I don't recommend our approach, but it *was* effective.

We both appreciate better the demands of true love. Paul brilliantly defines these demands in 1 Corinthians 13, but they are only words until life hands you an ultimatum to practice them. Now they have become our standards for marital behavior.

For a time, Jerry and Judy showed the effects of our fights by exhibiting increased belligerency and irritability in their personalities. This had been a difficult and even terrifying period in their lives. By explanation, but mostly by demonstrated love for them and for each other, we have gradually managed to restore that sense of security so important to children.

Our marriage and our family were most affected and threatened by all that happened. Restoring an atmosphere of love and trust and security in our home has had first priority ever since. By the grace of God, we have had success.

We still attend the same church regularly. Barbara has gained a new respect for Reverend Fellows since learning of the very important role he played in our reconciliation. I don't believe there is any question in her mind now that he is a man well acquainted with the Holy Spirit, a fact I always believed. Barbara is teaching a seventh-grade Sunday-school class this year; I haven't yet returned to the classroom.

Our adult Sunday-school class disbanded. Some of the Neo-Pentecostal members decided they would be happier in a church more closely aligned with their new beliefs. Naturally this was their privilege. The remaining members were absorbed by other classes.

Occasional meetings are still held in our Fellowship

Hall by the Pentecostal prayer groups. They are not forbidden nor intimidated by our church government. Speaking in tongues is not a part of our regular worship services, however, though several other innovations have been adopted to relieve the formality of the program.

To my knowledge, and it seems almost miraculous, we have lost no friends in the wake of our upheaval. Though Frank and Celia Beecham have moved on to another church, we are not alienated from them. Holly, Barbara's leader, had left with her husband much earlier to operate their Christian retreat in another state. Relations had always remained amicable with Murray Simms and Betty, our neighbor, even through the worst of the storm. I'm sure the Neo-Pentecostals we know feel more comfortable with Barbara than with me, but there is no hostility.

What, then, do we now believe about the Charismatic Movement? Barbara and I both have shifted our positions without entirely changing our minds. More shifting may occur as time goes by and some things become clearer to us.

Barbara finally finished John Kildahl's book, but she has done no other reading since. The total experience generated so much painful emotion in her that she wants to set aside for a while further study. Presently, she occupies essentially a neutral position. Conceding that both sides make good points for their contentions, she has decided for now to leave the controversy to others.

I personally still have many points of disagreement

with the Pentecostal and Neo-Pentecostal beliefs. Primarily these involve the Baptism in the Holy Spirit and the speaking in unknown tongues. But these concepts no longer panic me as they did in the beginning. Now they seem of no greater consequence than disagreements over sprinkling and total immersion forms of baptism, the use of musical instruments in worship services, the open or restricted Communion observance, or the like. They are denominational differences unworthy of the grotesque emphasis I placed upon them originally.

As my prejudice drained away, I found that in most respects I *agreed* with Charismatic positions. For instance, I totally agree that people today hunger and thirst for the living Christ and the joy, peace, and spiritual power that come from the indwelling Holy Spirit. I agree that Christ is concerned about our everyday problems and is both willing and able to help us in this life. I agree that if formalism or outdated liturgy weakens or even blocks the work of the Holy Spirit, then changes must be made (but not necessarily those prescribed by the Charismatic authors I have read). I even agree with the contention that our bodies and minds can be healed spiritually if God so desires; there is solid scriptural basis for spiritual healing from our Lord Himself, and many spiritual healings have been documented.

The agreements overwhelm the differences for a very simple reason: we serve the same Lord. It is Jesus who is important; that is, after all, why we are called Christians. As we climb Mount Zion by different paths it is only natural that we will see different scenery, but the distination is the same. If we keep our eyes on Jesus Christ at the summit, in-transit distractions will not bother us.

I know now that God used the Charismatic Movement to reveal some distressing things about me to myself. You see, prior to these experiences I'd thought I was a pretty good Christian. I tithed, I worshiped regularly, I taught Sunday school and led a teen-age prayer group, I had witnessed for Jesus in some difficult situations, and I daily asked for guidance and tasks from my Lord. I even prayed for God to make me more like Jesus.

Well, Jesus was perfect and Bob Branch was not, and God could see just where he wasn't. But after all, I had asked. Peter Marshall once gave a sermon entitled "Praying is Dangerous Business"; he was right.

As I put down these words, I am still appalled by what God saw in me. Over the space of a few months He revealed that I was entirely capable of doing the following things:

I withheld love from my wife and children.
I felt great prejudice toward anyone who spoke in unknown tongues.
I feared tongue speakers.
I practiced no tolerance toward my wife's new beliefs.
I wanted vengeance on those who led her to those beliefs.
I believed my wife was lying to me.

I couldn't forgive.

I sought my own solutions without consulting God.

Some Christian, huh?

Bob Branch is still not perfect and no one knows it better than he. He learns, though, and he's much more careful now to leave the driving to his Lord.

12

A More Excellent Way

Are there ways for others to avoid the anguish we suffered? Oh yes, and many readers will have already detected several of them. In closing, however, I would like to summarize my thoughts on this matter by offering a six-point plan of action. In writing this plan I assume the reader has had little or no contact with the Charismatic Movement before now. Here is the plan:

1. Be aware of the Charismatic Movement's existence and realize that because of its tremendous success it will probably touch your life at some time in the future.

2. Study the beliefs of the Charismatics and learn all you can about them. A short bibliography is included at the end of this book to get you started.

3. Talk to other Christians around you about the Movement and find out what they believe. Talk also with your pastor or priest.

4. After your study is complete, seek the Lord's guidance in making your own decision regarding the Movement.

5. Once your decision is made, be tolerant of the beliefs of others.

6. Practice love as you've never practiced it before!

Norman Vincent Peale is a preacher in whom I have great respect. He talks Christianity on a practical level that holds appeal for men and especially, I suppose, for technically trained men. One of his sermons dealt with the solution of problems, and in it he claimed that the seeds of the solution to every problem are contained within the problem itself. You only have to examine the problem very closely, he claims, to get the proper idea of how to solve it.

Nothing could have been truer in our case. Much of the scriptural basis for speaking in unknown tongues is contained in chapters twelve and fourteen of I Corinthians. Between the two, almost as if Paul had anticipated the trouble we would have, is the "still more excellent way," the way of perfect love. I could not fully appreciate this definition of true love until I had been under emotional stress almost beyond my capacity to bear. I hope that you can appreciate it sooner and avoid our ordeal.

Through grace I did not lose my wife and family as at one point I thought I might, but a loss *was* incurred and a serious one at that. While we bickered and fought and stewed over our differences, our share of the work of Christ went undone. Several weeks of time were lost for the Kingdom.

Never has there been a time in our history when Christ has been more desperately needed than now. The work load is tremendous and Christians can ill afford to fight among themselves and neglect it. In James 1:20 we are told that ". . . the anger of man does not work the righteousness of God." Our story painfully reflects the truth of that statement.

So if there are readers who have already taken some of my missteps, who are currently estranged from some of their fellow Christians for whatever reasons, please listen to these words from Saint Paul. They are a part of one of his great calls for unity and they are timeless. From Ephesians 4:31, 32: "Let all bitterness and wrath and anger and clamor and slander be put away from you, with all malice, and be kind to one another, tenderhearted, forgiving one another, as God in Christ forgave you."

Our time is now. Won't you please do that?

Bibliography

Advocating Books

Basham, Don. *Face Up With a Miracle*. Monroeville, Pennsylvania: Whitaker Books, 1971.

Bennett, Dennis J. *Nine O'Clock in the Morning*. Plainfield, New Jersey: Logos International, 1970.

Boone, Pat. *A New Song*. Carol Stream, Illinois: Creation House, Inc., 1970.

Brumback, Carl. *What Meaneth This?* A Pentecostal Answer to a Pentecostal Question. Springfield, Missouri: Gospel Publishing House, 1947.

Christenson, Larry. *Speaking in Tongues*. Minneapolis, Minnesota: Bethany Fellowship, Inc., 1968.

Ranaghan, Kevin and Dorothy. *Catholic Pentecostals*. Paramus, New Jersey: Paulist Newman Press, 1969.

Sherrill, John L. *They Speak With Other Tongues*. Old Tappan, New Jersey: Fleming H. Revell Company, 1965.

Dissenting Books

Burdick, Donald W. *Tongues: To Speak or Not to Speak.* Chicago, Illinois: Moody Press, 1969.

Cutten, George Barton. *Speaking With Tongues.* Historically and Psychologically Considered. New Haven, Connecticut: Yale University Press, 1927.

Gromacki, Robert G. *The Modern Tongues Movement.* Nutley, New Jersey: Presbyterian and Reformed Publishing Company, 1972.

Hoekema, Anthony A. *What About Tongue-Speaking?* Grand Rapids, Michigan: William B. Eerdmans Publishing Company, 1966.

_____. *Holy Spirit Baptism.* Grand Rapids, Michigan: William B. Eerdmans Publishing Company, 1972.

Kildahl, John P. *The Psychology of Speaking in Tongues.* New York, New York: Harper & Row, Publishers, 1972.

Stott, John R. W. *The Baptism & Fullness of the Holy Spirit.* Downers Grove, Illinois: Inter-Varsity Press, 1964.